FINDING
THE
SECRET
PLACE

To Jeni, chosen!
Your Father God draws
you "in" to His love
in the S.P. Then He
"leads" you OUT to
"do battle"! Praise
God for your willing
heart! ♡
    Emily Gardner Foppe
    Exodus Retreat
    9-22-17

Praise for *Finding the Secret Place*

I have believed and taught for a long time now that all things necessary for life are found in God's presence. Fullness of joy, perfect peace, absence of fear, unexplainable love, freedom from agitating moral conflicts, and abundant life are found in God's presence, for he is the true source of them all. Emily does an excellent job of simplifying the problem most of us have in obtaining these realities and clearly lays out a successful path to truly experience them. Emily shares simple yet profound truths that will bring the freedom and fulfillment to your life that you are looking for. Not only are her insights and instructions powerful and effective, but they are working in her life personally. I highly recommend *Finding the Secret Place*. You will be blessed as you read this book!

—DANON WINTER, director of Charis Bible College Florida;
pastor of Momentum Church in Jacksonville

Emily Gardner Foppe has triumphed over her personal struggles and has translated her steps to victory as a guide to anyone seeking the fullness of freedom through God. Her allegorical poem and simple steps, along with study questions, make this a refreshing way to view and attain your best, most intimate relationship with God. These eight keys—realize, reroute, receive, release, renew, redirect, rejoice, and repeat—will be music to your ears and water to your spirit!

—LEE ANN RUMMELL, chair of the board,
Christian Healing Ministries

God is always trying to get our attention. *Finding the Secret Place* is a story of Emily beginning to notice God's attempts to speak to her. It is a story of restoring her to life upon her commitment to value her relationship with God first and foremost in her life. It is a story of being at peace with God's new covenant of grace, love, and forgiveness, outside of the bondage of old-covenant, performance-based living. It is a story of Emily stepping out of her past and seeing and accepting a different future with Jesus as her redeemer and the Holy Spirit as her guide to God's plan for her life. *Finding the Secret Place* is a testament to God's love for Emily and her finding and embracing that love. It is God's desired story for each of us.

—BOB MASSEY, president of Massey Properties, Jacksonville, FL

Much of Emily Gardner Foppe's journey into a deeper intimacy with God and the discoveries she made along the way paralleled my own walk with the Lord, being moved by his Spirit from external and superficial religiosity to internal transformation through suffering, and coming to realize that my relationship with Jesus Christ, and his substitutionary atonement, supersedes everything. I appreciate Emily's passion and desire to help others navigate the sometimes muddy waters of the Christian faith. And I pray that many will benefit from Finding the Secret Place, that hearts and minds will become more devoted, more committed, more surrendered, and more submitted.

—WENDY DIETRICH, Messianic Jew, and Bible study teacher

FINDING THE SECRET PLACE

8 Keys to
Experiencing
God's Presence

EMILY GARDNER FOPPE

Finding the Secret Place: 8 Keys to Experiencing God's Presence
© 2016 by Emily Gardner Foppe
Published by Deep River Books
Sisters, Oregon
www.deepriverbooks.com

Unless otherwise noted, all Scriptures are taken from the Holy Bible, New Living Translation, Copyright © 1996, 2004, 2007 by Tyndale House Foundation. Used by permission of Tyndale House Publishers, Inc., Carol Stream, Illinois 60188. All rights reserved.

Scriptures marked "KJV" are taken from the King James Version of the Bible.

Scriptures marked "AMP" taken from the Amplified® Bible, Copyright © 2015 by The Lockman Foundation. Used by permission. (www.lockman.org)

ISBN: 9781632694195
Library of Congress: 2016950121

Printed in the USA
Cover design by Robin Black, Inspirio Design

CONTENTS

POEM: The Shells. 11

INTRODUCTION: Right? 15

CHAPTER 1: Realize 19

CHAPTER 2: Reroute 29

CHAPTER 3: Receive 39

CHAPTER 4: Release 55

CHAPTER 5: Renew. 71

CHAPTER 6: Redirect. 87

CHAPTER 7: Rejoice 103

CHAPTER 8: Repeat. 115

AFTERWORD: Rest. 131

8 Keys to Experiencing God's Presence 137

Answers 139

Scripture Verses for Discussion Questions 149

To my mom and dad, Mary Ann and Charles Elyea, who raised me up in the church and laid the groundwork for who I am today. You always did your very best. I miss you so much. I love you always and look forward to seeing you again!

To my children, Kate, Will and Claire. If it hadn't been for you I wouldn't know nearly as much! I love you to the moon! Thank you for loving and supporting me through all the "twists and turns"! Can't wait to see what happens next with you and all your little families. It is all good!

To Larry! You are such an unexpected surprise and delight! If it weren't for you this book would likely never have happened. I love you so much, and I thank God for you every day!

THE SHELLS

Two conch shells nestled,
hidden under cover of predawn sky.
Magnetized by the moon,
they drew my feet nigh,
to the secret place in the slipping tide,
where I would have eyes to see,
and truth could no longer hide.

I had already run too many miles.
Lost in a sea of thoughts
about love gone awry
and life's crooked wiles.
Shoes continuously pounding.
Body moving with sway.
I nimbly moved past an errant wave.
Then my thoughts gave way!

No calm in this breaking day,
until repentance.
Change your direction!
Let God have His Perfect Say!

My pace faltered.

Was that God's nudging I had perceived?
Did I hear right?
From this crushing storm I could be relieved?

Another thought my own mind conceived:
If I relent to the Lord,
I will never again be love-deceived!
The Spirit is giving me ears to hear—
and a heart that truly believes!

Then I heard a whisper:
"There is a man whose heart is huge.
And you he will lead."

And so I ran harder toward the dawn's new light.
Sure that God would grant wisdom, peace, and might.
The promise of a man who would do what is right—
who knows His name and will be my armored knight.
A man who will find in me trustworthiness, adoration, and delight.

No more sidestepping!
I was abiding.
Trusting Him to ease my plight!

And so the tide receded.
And the shells came into sight.

They lay side by side in the sand,
like two lovers.
One, a third the size of the other.
They reflected the conversation
God and I had just had with one another!

Abruptly, I stopped to gaze at these two souls,
connecting, confiding.
The larger with the greater voice:

the protector and defender,
the leader of choice.

"But when will I find him?
This marathon has caused injury, mistakes.
Surely, soon, the man of Your choosing
will appear in my life space!
Indeed, the man who has the endurance needed
to help me finish this race!"

I lingered, hoping His answer would yield
more than a trace.

Then He spoke.
And I heard His voice Godspeed!
"My daughter, you are in bondage to the notion
that a mortal man is all you need!
I am the larger shell!
Your Husband,
Defender,
Protector,
Lover and Friend!

Learn to trust Me above all others
in this life.
Then I will send,
the man of your dreams to you.
On this, My Word, you can depend.
So I am preparing the man
who will support this dictate.
But to finish the work I began in you,
we must wait.
You see, I granted Satan permission
to sift you as wheat!

But that drove you to repentance,
baptism, and release!

Soon you will teach your sisters
the story of the shells.
How when they trust Me first,
their fears and burdens
are released and dispelled.
So teach them how to run to Me to be safe!
That My name is their strong tower.
That when they come to Me,
they receive favor and power.

Now, with that Word spoken,
you go and bless others.
I'll be taking care of the rest!"

And so I gathered the shells,
and held them tight to my chest.
Love tokens to have and to hold,
while I wait for His best.

PS
I departed with a bonfire heart,
ignited by the Holy Spirit spark!
And I am free indeed!
Lord, I do trust You!
You give me everything I need!

EMILY E. GARDNER
February 18, 2014
This poem was inspired by a run on the beach in November 2013.

RIGHT?

There is a path before each person that seems right,
but it ends in death.
PROVERBS 14:12

THE REVELATION I RECEIVED from "The Shells" had been coming to me over several years' time. But it was that day and through that visual experience that I was ready to receive it. I was up early, running on the beach, my usual routine—a dark, uninterrupted time of thinking my deepest, most selfish thoughts. For the last three months, my inner life had been a constant stream of heartbroken me, me, me thoughts. I asked myself the same question over and over again: Why would God hold out on giving me the One Thing I had always wanted? I had been stuck in the same thought pattern for decades, though I was unaware of it.

Now, I'm an optimist. And somewhat of a perfectionist. And a moralist. So I had always tried to live my best life. The Bible says there is a way that "seems right" to a man, and it sure seemed to me that I was going about it right. But the path was not straight. There were many disappointments and frustrations, twists and turns, especially leading up to my divorce after twenty-three years of marriage. Then for nine years as a single person, I marched around and around the mountain—never getting any closer to where I was supposed to go.

Friend, if you can relate to my story, you have also suffered from a nagging disappointment, a problem you can't get over, or perhaps an addiction that you cannot fix. And it has consumed too much of your energy, dominated too much of your thought life, and kept you down, broken, limited, and restricted. In other words, your life has, to some degree, been robbed of purpose, peace, and freedom.

I wrote "The Shells" for my own edification. I simply wanted to document the revelation God had given me so I would never forget it. All those years I thought I had put Him first in my life—only to realize that He was always second to the One Thing, in this case my desire for a human husband who could and would meet my deepest needs. I finally got it. Once I trusted God *first* to meet my needs, I was able to get unstuck in my thoughts, my emotions, and the trajectory of my life.

Almost by accident, I began sharing "The Shells" with friends and acquaintances. It occurred to me that the story often hit a nerve with readers, stirring deep emotion. It seemed that what was so personal to me had almost universal relevance.

I decided to write this book to explain the underlying biblical principles in the poem. These are the principles I had been thinking about and studying and seeking to apply for several years prior to my encounter with God on the beach. So dear reader, if you are stuck in life, I wrote this book for you. Follow the recipe, and you will discover a truly "right" way to do life that is satisfying and purposeful, even exciting and fun! You will find peace and freedom. God is so good! He loves us. He is patient. He always gives us exactly what we need.

Personal Reflections

1. On a scale of 1 to 10 (10 being the greatest) what is your current level of purpose? Peace? Freedom?

2. Do you feel stuck on anything in your thoughts, emotions, or direction? Do you constantly see or focus upon something from the past or present that keeps you stuck, such as a problem, person,

addiction, or situation that holds you back, distracts you, and even consumes you?

3. What is your greatest disappointment in life?

CHAPTER 1

REALIZE

Ears to hear and eyes to see. Both are gifts from the LORD.
PROVERBS 20:12

Key #1: If we are stuck and consumed by problems, the life we live is not the one God intended—but a much higher level of living can be discovered and experienced. To begin discovering that life, we must REALIZE the greatest truths about God and His archenemy, Satan, the deceiver of our souls.

I'VE HAD A NUMBER OF REALIZATIONS about God in my lifetime, the most significant ones always coming through experiences that were visual in some way or another. You have probably seen and heard a door slam. You've seen (maybe not used!) a tube of red lipstick. And it's likely you have seen conch shells lying on a sandy beach. Just ordinary things, to most people. But these images are forever extraordinary and personal to me because they came to me at crucial moments in time when I sensed that God was trying to have a conversation, and He used visuals to reinforce what He was saying so I would know it was Him—so I would engage in the conversation and then remember. Spiritual exclamation points, if you will, spanning thirty-six years. The last occurred when I wrote "The Shells."

I have not always been able to say this emphatically, but now I can: God has been pursuing me for a very long time. I haven't always listened. And I haven't always remembered everything that He has said. But I have always remembered the exclamation points. And the exclamation points got me to where I am today—unstuck!

And so I want to share the principles I have learned with you, in hopes that you will develop eyes to see what He is doing and ears to hear what He is saying in your own life. God loves you and wants to have many conversations with you about things that are important to Him and to you. Even now, He is reaching down and touching your life in such a way that speaks to your heart only. You are special in His sight, and He wants to involve you in His Big Story. Even now, at this very moment, He is showing you new things! You are developing a new, broadening perspective. You are rising up! You are starting to see things from a much higher elevation. And you know this is from Him! It is becoming so obvious to you now.

"For I am about to do something new. See, I have already begun!
Do you not see it? I will make a pathway through the wilderness.
I will create rivers in the dry wasteland."
ISAIAH 43:19

The Two Trees

There are many things we need to realize about God if we are to know Him and get unstuck in our lives. For starters, we must understand this: if we are stuck and consumed by problems, the life we live is not the one God intended. He intended that we live a supernatural, eternal life on Earth in perfect, harmonious, intimate friendship with Him. God intended Paradise: the same life He created for mankind in the beginning.

There is an image in the Bible for such a life: the Tree of Life. It was a real, fruit-bearing tree among many others in the middle of the garden where creation began. But it was not ordinary. It had special, life-giving, eternal properties. To ingest its fruit was to ingest the very heart of God Himself—His love, His goodness, His generosity, His essence.

And so, because God is love, because He is good, because He is a giver, because He is forever heart-motivated and relational, His Spirit created man and woman with this highest level of existence in mind, set apart from the rest of creation. They were the highest level beings in creation, made from God's own DNA, bearing his own character and likeness.

Then God breathed the breath of life into the first man and woman, and they lived as beings in three dimensions—spirit, soul, and body— living vessels through which God's love and power flowed.

God made humans, in part, from the same substance He used to make the angels—His own Spirit! We share the same DNA, the same Divine Nature Ability, as God and the angels! Therefore, we are equipped to perform at a supernatural level!

Angels are . . . spirits sent to care for people
who will inherit salvation.
HEBREWS 1:14

Yet you made them [humans] only a little lower than the angels
and crowned them with glory and honor.
PSALM 8:5

This message is from the LORD,
who stretched out the heavens, laid the foundations
of the earth, and formed the human spirit.
ZECHARIAH 12:1

Now may the God of peace make you holy in every way,
and may your whole spirit and soul and body be kept blameless
until our Lord Jesus Christ comes again.

1 THESSALONIANS 5:23

Adam and Eve knew God intimately, understood Him completely, and were heart-motivated just like Him, just as He had intended. So God delegated to them power and authority over all of creation. Life on Earth was peaceful, restful, and purposeful. God's Spirit was the supplier of all good things. Adam and Eve had everything they needed.

But when God bestows blessing and favor, responsibility follows. Indeed, He had blessed Adam and Eve beyond measure, giving them dominion over the Earth and the freedom to make choices. But He required One Thing. Whereas He had encouraged them to eat from the Tree of Life, there was another tree in the middle of the garden from which they were not to eat: the Tree of Knowledge of Good and Evil. God had commanded Adam, "Do not eat the fruit of this tree or you will surely die!"

Now there was a Serpent in the garden who had no power or authority over the earth—neither in the physical nor the spiritual realm of God's creation. But the Serpent's modus operandi was to deceive, for he represented evil. And evil did exist in the universe, though not yet on Earth or in the minds and hearts of Adam and Eve, who were motivated by God's love only, nothing else. This is why God commanded them not to eat of the tree that would give them knowledge of evil. To do so would give them understanding that emanated from a dark place in another realm. And that understanding would destroy their heart motivation, which would change everything.

So the Serpent came alongside Eve. And he beguiled her into thinking that God didn't really love her and that He was purposely withholding something from her—something she "needed" so as to be more like Him. Most certainly, she must eat of this forbidden tree to get what she needed.

In that instant, the Serpent managed to shift Eve's focus from what God had done and given her to the One Thing she had not been allowed to have. Almost without hesitation, she ate. Then she distracted Adam. He lost his focus too, and ate with her. Immediately, their hearts became subservient to their minds, and they were filled with negative, harmful thoughts—all lies.

In this book, the "One Thing" is anything in life that causes harm or stymies spiritual growth. It might even be something that is ostensibly good. Most humans have at least One Thing that fits this description. What was Eve's One Thing at this time? What was God's intention or objective here? What does His intention signify to you?

The Pursuit

"Where are you?" God asked the question when He walked in the garden after Adam and Eve ate from the tree. Of course this was a rhetorical question. He knew exactly where Adam and Eve were hiding. Having eaten from the tree, they had realized their nakedness, becoming "self" conscious. Suddenly everything in their lives seemed confused and out of control! They had lost their power and authority! So they ran and attempted to hide from God, who was pursing them.

But God came to them. And there they were, crouching and covered in fig leaves—not resembling anything He had created them to be. Before, Adam and Eve's hearts had been conduits of His infinite love, which had poured forth from them like gushing rivers. Now their minds were dominant—and twisted—controlling their self-centered, self-defensive, self-preserving, and self-sufficient hearts. Adam and Eve's disobedience had foiled the plan God intended for them on Earth. They had willfully yielded their God-given authority to the Serpent. Evil had then entered the earth, forcing oppression, self-centeredness, distrust, and all kinds of other problems upon the hearts and minds of men.

Now, the character and nature and integrity of God never change. So when God granted power, authority, and freedom to physical human beings, He was bound by His Word to uphold those things. Even when Adam and Eve mishandled their responsibility and got themselves into a real jam, God could not just change things up and renege on the gifts He had given them. Understand: He certainly had the power and authority to do that if He wanted, but His integrity would not allow it.

So it was because of His love and His great mercy that God formulated a plan of action that did meet His integrity requirement. It was an intricate, yet very simple plan—one that could ultimately restore human beings back to their original value and identity as heart-motivated beings who would again manifest God's love and power.

The pursuit was on! No doubt, God's creative abilities and processes would be needed to get the job done.

There are two Hebrew words in the Bible used to describe God's creative process. *Bara* means to "create something out of nothing." *Asah* means "to create or make out of existing material." Most theologians argue that both words connote an instantaneous and supernatural creation. Many say *bara* is the verb emphasized as regards the creation of the heavens and earth, the sea creatures and birds, and man.

In the beginning God created [bara] the heavens and the earth.
GENESIS 1:1

So God created [bara] great sea creatures and every living
thing that scurries and swarms in the water, and every sort
of bird—each producing offspring of the same kind.
And God saw that it was good.
GENESIS 1:21

So God created [bara] human beings in his own image.
In the image of God he created them;
male and female he created them.
GENESIS 1:27

In the same way that God created the original heavens and Earth out of nothing, He is able to supernaturally create new things in your life and mine, even out of nothing. This was His plan since the beginning. It is the way He restores us to our "rightness" with Him! Only then can we solve life's problems, get our hurts healed, and find and live out our God-ordained purpose!

Back to the Beginning

God has loved us with an everlasting love since the beginning of time. He has always wanted to have an intimate relationship with us, His creations. He intended a life for us here on Earth which existed for only a short time. But then man fell due to his rebellion. His heart-motivation was displaced by a quest for ultimate knowledge, and his God-given authority and power over creation was yielded to the devil. But God's love compelled Him to pursue us. He knew a way He could restore us back to our original state without violating His integrity.

So God kept talking to anyone who would listen. He kept using visual images so we wouldn't forget. He unveiled a plan. Then He showed us how we can participate, not only returning to our original purpose ourselves but also becoming His touch and His voice to others. We still live in a fallen world, but we can rise high above it. We can thrive, not just get by! The more we have ears to hear and eyes to see, the closer we get to living the life He intended. Salvation is not just going to heaven. It is to bringing heaven back to Earth! We can receive this! We can live at the highest level!

"I am the Lord, the God of all the peoples of the world.
Is anything too hard for me?"
Jeremiah 32:27

Discussion Questions

Look up the Scriptures listed and reflect on the questions presented. Possible "answers", along with Scripture references from the New Living Translation, can be located at the back of this book.

1. What has been God's intention for humanity since the beginning? (Genesis 1:10, 12, 22, 28, 31; Psalm 37:23–24; Romans 8:28; Genesis 2:18; Jeremiah 29:11; Luke 24:50–51)

2. What did the Tree of Life offer Adam and Eve? (Genesis 2:9; Revelation 22:1–5)

3. Why was the Tree of Knowledge of Good and Evil so bad for them? (Genesis 2:16–17)

4. How did God set man apart from the rest of creation? (Job 33:4; Genesis 1:26; Psalm 8:3–6; Genesis 2:15–17) Why do you think God made us?

5. How does God feel about us on an emotional level? (Psalm 23:6; Psalm 139:7, 17; Isaiah 43:1–4)

Personal Reflections

1. God can supernaturally create things in our lives even out of nothing—just as He did in the beginning when He spoke the heavens and Earth, the sea creatures and birds, and man into existence. If you could get rid of the One Thing, would you be able to see

the New Thing that God is creating "out of nothing" in you? What might your New Thing be?

2. How does it make you feel to know that you cannot hide from God—that He is constantly pursuing you? Do you think of it as an invasion of privacy? Or is it comforting to know that God is constantly thinking of you and that He loves you?

3. God is creating something for you that is good and satisfying. Will you let Him? Do you believe there is anything too difficult for Him?

CHAPTER 2

REROUTE

"The Kingdom of God is near! Repent of your sins and believe the Good News!"
MARK 1:15

Key #2: We are born into enemy territory, displaced, and disconnected from God's love. So we must REROUTE—turn from our own way of living life and follow His lead. When we make a conscious decision to do this, we become connected to His Spirit power and can begin hearing His voice.

YOU'VE HEARD IT STATED—to get to where you want to go, start with the end in mind. Then work backward. If you happen to get off track, immediately reroute. And pay attention! If you get more than a little off course, you will likely suffer the loss of valuable time and energy. And if you meander around and end up too far from the intended destination, you may never have the incentive to get back on course. So never, ever take your eyes off of the end.

An internal GPS with a strong connection to God's Spirit—a system like the one Adam and Eve enjoyed in the beginning—is critical for a person who desires to live successfully at the highest level. For Adam and Eve, all was in working order until they fell into rebellion, took their eyes off God, and turned into enemy territory. That's when their spirits malfunctioned and they lost connection to the Server.

In one fell swoop, humans separated from God's Spirit, were banished from the garden, and were cut off from the Tree of Life, finding themselves suddenly mortal, displaced, and disconnected. This also meant they were cut off from God's love, which created a huge void in their hearts. And they were keenly aware of this void and desperate to fill it—for without His love they could not survive. With no direction and no connection, they wandered aimlessly, looking for love in all the wrong places.

Obviously, this was not the end God had in mind for them. Remember, God is love. And He had created humans with Divine Nature Ability! We were made to manifest His love—to *be* love.

So God's Spirit was bound to find a way to reconnect our spirits to His, the only way we could again manifest His Life in and through our own. But to accomplish that end, He needed to bring heaven's power and love back to Earth. And to do that, He had to work within the constraints of a fallen world. In other words, God would not alter or diminish man's free will to accomplish His end, His goal, though He would use various supernatural means to woo mankind back to Himself. Ultimately, we humans had to very deliberately reroute, change our minds, and turn to follow Him. Then God's messages could be received—and the plot to the Big Story could unfold.

The Reset Button

So God sent His Spirit out into the earth. But full human access to God's life, love, and power would not occur until the climax of the Big Story. And a lot of story had to happen before that time would fully come! You see, the collective consciousness of man had become increasingly evil and sin-sick due to the nature of human rebellion. Spirit reception was almost nil—at most, a flicker. The human race had nearly forgotten Him.

But God was formulating a way to create something out of nothing! He had already determined that He must push the reset button to save mankind from themselves and move the Big Story along. He needed but one human spirit to respond to His call and agree to join Him in His work. That man would be the one to help save the human race and usher in new life and beginnings.

Noah was the man who responded. At first he perceived only a nudge, deep within his consciousness. But he paid attention! Then the nudge became a force, drawing him. So he followed it. Amazingly, it seemed this force was a loving, approachable, and knowable Being!

Noah sensed that his life was about to radically change. Then he realized he was walking in a direction opposite of where everyone else on Earth was going! Immediately, his spirit receiver began recharging, the connection to God's Spirit getting stronger and stronger! All of a sudden, He could hear God's voice—loud and clear!

So God spoke to Noah and told him what He was planning to do. He was going to send a flood that would devastate all life on Earth and thereby wipe out all evil. It seemed harsh. But God knew He must do this to turn things on Earth around. Otherwise, the human race would completely self-destruct.

After the flood, a remnant of strong receivers who could start afresh and work to bring the Big Story to a climax would be needed. This would include Noah, his family, and one pair of all living creatures then inhabiting the earth.

Noah's job was to build a giant boat that would protect the remnant during the great storm—a project that would require extreme focus, dedication, and receptivity to God's instruction. No human had built a ship that size—one-and-a-half football fields long and four stories high! No small undertaking for the first nautical engineer!

But Noah answered yes to the call God gave him. And for one hundred twenty years, the construction of that giant boat on dry land was a visual statement of God's plan. We can only imagine that many passersby had the opportunity to change their minds and join in. But no one did. Probably most were apathetic. Other naysayers likely gathered around the ark from time to time to distract Noah and ridicule the execution of God's plan. No doubt, Noah took every opportunity to warn them. His message: Reroute! Pay attention! Change direction!

Noah remained faithful to the project until it was completed. God gave him the wisdom and encouragement he needed. Then God rounded up the animals. The rains came down, and Noah's family and all the creatures entered the ark and survived the flood. The first reset in the Big Story was complete. God promised Noah's progeny that He would never again destroy the earth by flood. The rainbow was a sign of the covenant He made.

Other Big Story resets would occur along the way in varying degrees and in different kinds—sometimes affecting the lives of individuals and other times the lives of many at once. We will discuss some of the other resets God initiated later in this book. But regardless of how and when God intervened in human lives and in history, His intentions have always been the same. To this day, resetting is often His way of getting our attention so that we will reroute and get out of our own way. Resets allow us to see Him more clearly, love Him more dearly, and follow Him more nearly! They enable us to have a vibrant relationship with Him and become active and effective participants in the rest of the Big Story!

The Big Story began when God created from nothing the
heavens and the earth and all there is in it, including
humans made in His image. The plot of the story continued
for a very long period of time, as God chose willing

participants to play critical roles. The point of no return, or climax, of the story occurred when Jesus—God's Son—shed blood, then resurrected from the dead. The plot continues, as all stories do, until the conclusion, when all the parts come together. At that point, everything that has happened in the Big Story will finally make sense!

The Slamming Door

I've had two official rerouting experiences in my lifetime. The first was when I was nineteen years old, and the second was around the time of the shells. Both experiences were equally significant. Both involved a change of mind and heart that immediately altered my behavior. Both times God revealed something I needed to know about myself that I had not been previously aware of. And both times He used visual images to make a point I have never forgotten.

Interestingly, I held totally different mindsets prior to each experience. So when God came to me in the garden on those two different occasions—and found me crouching and covered in fig leaves—He came at me from totally different angles. But both times He told me what I needed to hear and in such a way that was best and for my own good at the time, so I would understand the need to reroute and could then be ready and able to receive what He was offering.

The Bible teaches that God is both kind and severe. The severity of God hates evil, which can also be defined as "sin and separation" from Himself. His perfection, His justice, and His integrity require that evil be dealt with according to a certain standard that has been set. His judgment of man at the time of the flood is an example of this aspect of His character. The fact that God pursues us even when we have rebelled and separated ourselves from Him is an example of His loving kindness.

At nineteen, I had been a churchgoer my whole life. My dad was a preacher! I had always believed in God. I had always believed that He loved me. I was good, moral, dutiful, conscientious, and over-achieving. And I'm sure I thought those things somehow made me right with Him, in relationship with Him and deserving of eternal salvation. But when I went away to college and met some people who knew Him as a trusted friend, I got worried. Their trees were bear-ing a lot of fruit that my tree didn't have. They actually cared about other people, they exuded God's love, and their faces were radiant! That was when I realized I had missed something—something ter-ribly important, though I wasn't sure exactly what.

Thank God for His loving kindness, which gently leads us to a change of mind, heart, and action! His intervention came rather unex-pectedly. And at the time, I wasn't altogether sure what was happen-ing. But later, when I looked back to that day, it was so obvious. It was the day I rerouted!

I had already read somewhere in the Bible the passage where appar-ent followers of God said, "Lord, Lord, didn't we do all these things in Your name?" And He replied and told them to depart because He did not know them. Other passages I read describe a day when the door to heaven will shut. Those on the outside will plead to get in, saying "Lord, Lord, open the door for us!" But it will be too late. He will answer, "I don't know you or where you come from."

I had never noticed these severity-of-God-type passages before. But there they were—sandwiched in with all the other ones that I had read about God's love and mercy. I was starting to hear the com-plete message. My morality and my belief system were not enough. Everything I represented was tainted and self-motivated. It had been all about me, nothing else. I had to change something, but what?

My thoughts about all of this had been building toward a crescendo when I happened to go home one weekend to visit my family. That Sunday afternoon I was in a very bad mood because my mother wanted me to attend a church meeting in a show of support to my dad. There had been an undercurrent of some kind in the church, and a few of the leaders were trying to stir things up. I didn't want to go because I had other things to do, which was selfish in itself. But there I was in the church, sulking and half-listening to the controversy, when suddenly the debate started getting more and more intense. I remember it all caught me totally off guard. Suddenly a leader was yelling at my dad, screeching his chair across the floor, pounding his feet.

BAM! He slammed the door as hard as he could.

Silence. What had just happened? We all sat in disbelief. I was shocked. My emotions starting boiling up inside me. *You hypocrite! You had no right to disrespect my dad like that!* My poor dad's face was anguished. He slumped over in his chair. I was so upset. The meeting ended soon after. I nearly ran across the yard to our house with the sound of a door slamming over and over again in my head. Finally, I threw myself down on my bed, sobbing, attempting to console myself to sleep, but to no avail. I felt horrible. I was so, so sorry that it had happened. So sorry that I had contributed to the negative atmosphere with my bad attitude! Sorry that my dad had to suffer. That people are so selfish, so misguided. I blubbered, "Lord, I do not want my life to be like this. Please save me from it! I've been pretending! I want to know You and follow You now! I want to be like the people I know at school! Please show me how!"

All About the Kingdom

The end to the Big Story is all about the kingdom of God, which includes the eternal life believers will ultimately experience in heaven. And salvation is the means to that end. To find the kingdom, we cannot overlook any of the keys, especially this one—reroute! Rerouting involves realizing our sin and separation from God, being sorry about it, and then changing our minds about what we will now do and the direction we will go.

Rerouting comes as a result of God's pursuit. Oftentimes God's kindness and love manifested in the lives of others prompts the change. Other times a passage in the Bible comes alive to us, or we hear a word in a one-to-one conversation with Him, or some combination of all three. It often comes through a small thing. But God's kindness is what leads us to a place where we have eyes to see and ears to hear the need for rerouting. The result is godly sorrow that leads us away from sin and selfishness and lays the groundwork for receiving salvation through faith or whatever change in direction we need. This is what happened to me at age nineteen.

Jesus said, "How can I describe the Kingdom of God?
What story should I use to illustrate it? It is like a mustard seed
planted in the ground. It is the smallest of all seeds, but it becomes
the largest of all garden plants; it grows long branches, and birds
can make nests in its shade." (Mark 4:30–32)

So don't be afraid, little flock. For it gives your Father great
happiness to give you the Kingdom. (Luke 12:32)

But the Good News about the kingdom of God is more than just eternal salvation! The kingdom is also "near"—a supernatural life on Earth, manifesting love, power, peace, joy, and freedom in the Holy Spirit. Such kingdom living is God's desire for all of us while we are here on Earth. This was His original intention. And this kind of heightened experience is available—to anyone who wants to receive it—through the transforming power of the Holy Spirit.

The religious people of Jesus's day, the Pharisees, had a difficult time understanding the concept of God's kingdom. One day they asked Jesus, "When will the kingdom of God come?" Jesus replied, "The kingdom of God can't be detected by visible signs. You won't be able to say, 'Here it is!' or 'It's over there!' For the kingdom of God is already among you"—i.e., the kingdom *is within you,* or *is in your grasp* (Luke 17:20–21, AMP).

My hope for any new believer is that she will grasp this life sooner rather than later. I, for one, hardly got past the first few steps of spiritual understanding and development until much later in life. Consequently, I lived way too long not knowing how to grow in the power of the Holy Spirit. Life's disappointments and discouragements had set in, and I got way off track. It took many years before my Spirit receiver was again strong enough to pick up the signals God had been constantly sending! But praise God, the time did come! I had never lost my salvation, but I did need to start over again—to reroute. More on that in a later chapter. For now, remember this: wherever you are at today, the kingdom of God is near—perhaps just one rerouting away!

Discussion Questions

Look up the Scriptures listed and reflect on the questions presented. Possible "answers", along with Scripture references from the New Living Translation, can be located at the back of this book.

1. What is God's nature? (Isaiah 54:10; 1 John 4:7–8; Zephaniah 3:17; Psalm 136:26; Psalm 86:15; Proverbs 3:11–12)

2. What is our nature as fallen human beings? How has it affected our relationship with God? (Isaiah 59:2; Psalm 51:5; Isaiah 53:6)

3. What is the Good News? (2 Peter 3:9; Isaiah 54:8; Psalm 51:17; 1 John 1:5–7; Jeremiah 29:13–14; 2 Corinthians 7:10)

4. God's love can be "severe." What happens when we do not turn and follow Him? (Romans 2:4–5; Romans 11:22; Romans 6:23)

5. The bottom line is this: God wants us to reroute and run to Him to be safe! (Proverbs 18:10; Proverbs 3:5–6). To do that, we must first trust His character. Based on what you have learned so far, what character traits make Him trustworthy?

Personal Reflections

1. What are your thoughts concerning the role you are playing in the Big Story? Is it the role you want? Do you want another? If you could rewrite your script, what would your role be?

2. Has there been anything in your life that you didn't understand—that you used as an excuse for lack of trust? Did you rebel against God, or run and hide? What do you need to trust Him for now? If you were able to really trust the situation to Him, how would that change things for you? How would things change for those around you?

CHAPTER 3:

RECEIVE

To all who believed Him and accepted Him,
He gave the right to become children of God.
JOHN 1:12

Key #3: God's plan has always involved partnering with ordinary people to accomplish His work so we humans could be bought back from the power of Satan and restored to our original state as sons and daughters. When we believe and RECEIVE the Good News about Jesus, our identity as God's children is reinstated, with all the rights and privileges thereof. We then have access to the power and love of God. Satan's power over us can be thwarted.

HUMANITY'S STORY AS WE SEE IT laid out in the Bible is replayed in each of our lives. We fall, sin, and hide. Then God's pursuit calls us to reroute, at which point He offers us the Good News of the kingdom —if we will believe and receive it. In other words, God established a way through which we could once again become His children—with all the rights and privileges thereof, namely the right to manifest His life, power, and love. It was a brilliant plan! It was the climax to the Big Story. But it would take a while to get to that point.

Remember, after Adam, God's unlimited power became limited—not because He could not do whatever He wanted, but because His integrity held Him to His His commitment to uphold man's freedom to choose. That meant He could only work through the faith of humans who believed His messages and were amenable to a partnership. And most humans were still in obeisance to the father of this world, Satan, who had been in control since the fall.

So when He was ready to do a new thing, God picked Abraham, whose receptors were fully functioning. Abraham heard God speak. And he believed what God had said. He trusted Him.

Then one day, God decided to test Abraham's faith with a radical message. He explained that the Big Story was unfolding, and that from that point forward, the main characters in the story's plot would be Abraham's biological descendants. God also promised that Abraham's descendants would forever be His treasured possession, His chosen people. In fact, He was going to bless the entire world through Abraham's family!

Now this was Good News—especially given the fact that Abraham and his wife, Sarah, were already very old, and she had never been able to conceive a child. But God pressed on. In the end, Abraham's children would include adopted sons and daughters. And his family would be so great in number that he could not even begin to fathom it.

All those years ago, God told Abraham to look up at the stars in the sky and to imagine the sand on the seashore. These images would help him come close to grasping the idea that he would become father to so many and would serve as reminders to the promise that God made.

So Abraham believed and received God's message and His instructions. By faith, he and Sarah were to pack their belongings and travel to a land that God would show them. They did not know for sure where they were going or how long it would take to get there. But God would guide and give them what they needed. Ultimately, He would give them a fertile land, a key factor in the Big Story, then the promised son, a grandson, and a great-grandson, all key players.

> *Jesus said, "Seek the Kingdom of God, above all else, and live righteously, and he will give you everything you need."*
> MATTHEW 6:33

After Abraham, there would be many other participants and critical events in the story. And the storyline wasn't always positive. Not surprisingly, the power of evil continued to be a dominant force with which the descendants reckoned. Down the line, there would be a great famine, then enslavement of Abraham's people in Egypt. Four hundred years later, there would be a miraculous release from that bondage and a very long and arduous journey back to the original land God had given them. Then came man-made administrations, and wars and evil goings-on, and prophetic warnings and announcements, and threats of annihilation. In total, these happenings would span another two thousand years! But the climax to the Big Story would come just as God said—through Abraham and Sarah's lineage and as a result of their initial faith and obedience.

God never lost sight of the goal of restoring humanity back to its original identity so that once again image-bearers like you and me could know Him intimately as sons and daughters and enjoy His peace and freedom.

Why did God pick Abraham? Not because he was perfect. He had faith. And he was agreeable to a partnership with God. But he rarely did things exactly according to God's specifications!

For example, twenty-five years after God made His promise to Abraham, Sarah had not yet conceived a child. To help the process along, Abraham superseded God's plans and had sexual relations with one of his servants. That servant bore Abraham a son, whose lineage evolved into the Arab people group, his nation's strongest opposition, even today.

But God never abandoned Abraham and his people, in spite of Abraham's waywardness! Nor did He abandon His purposes for them—or for any of His partners who have believed and received since that day. Without fail, God continues to work in and around the foibles of those He chooses.

We can ask the same question of ourselves as we do about Abraham. Why did God pick me? He wanted to transform my broken image. He wanted me, His fallen creature, to be a daughter who manifests His life-giving, transforming power. But it would be a long, long process. I had been a child of God for more than a decade before I even began to realize what a radical transformation God intended for my life.

For the Lord your God is the God of gods and Lord of lords. He is the great God, the mighty and awesome God, who shows no partiality and cannot be bribed.
DEUTERONOMY 10:17

I will cry to God Most High, who accomplishes all things on my behalf (for He completes my purpose in His Plan).
PSALM 57:2, AMP

The Outside-In Problem

To develop His plan in my life, first, God had to deal with me on a few of the basics. I had received the Good News. But I had way too much head knowledge for my own good! In the first ten years of my Christian life, I was a member and leader of my college's Christian fellowship and taught junior high English at a Christian school. I completed an intensive two-year course on the Bible. I had rarely, if ever, missed church on Sunday. And of course, I was involved with numerous small groups over the years. If that wasn't enough, I also led a weekly outreach Bible study for ladies in my neighborhood!

In other words, it was ten years of going through the motions and doing a lot of the "right" stuff. But it was an outside-in performance gospel—and I was exhausted. Not only that, I was miserable! I had done all the work to be the kind of Christian I thought I should be, yet my world was falling apart.

First and foremost, my marriage was strained and had been for quite some time. My husband's main concern in life was always his business, which had been suffering for several years. Finances were dire. Also, the kids were having some issues. Dad needed to be more involved. I needed help! And yet my husband couldn't deliver.

I felt abandoned. I just couldn't make sense of any of it. I had done all the right things! All I had ever wanted in life was a close, intimate marriage and a happy home. Not riches! Just happiness! But my dream was being lost. I sensed that it was slipping through my fingers. Nonetheless, I tried to stand tall and hold it all together.

Around this same time, I had a neighbor whose children were similar ages to mine. Our interaction was mainly due to the kids, but we were friends at a distance, probably because I was overtly Christian and she was Jewish. She called herself a "secular Jew" and didn't attend synagogue. I viewed her as unsaved but good—very thoughtful and kind.

Well, her goodness really tripped me up! I thought I knew "the truth," and I knew she didn't have it. And I did try to share my faith with her. At one point we had a couple of very good, one-sided conversations! I did all the talking. Her response: *Whatever works for you!* And that really bugged me.

Then a thought crept in. *Lord, here I am serving you—and yet when it comes right down to it, what do I have to show for it? How am I really any better off than she is?* I'm sure I knew the right answers to these questions, but my thinking was emotional, cloudy, complicated. She seemed to have a life that was more together than mine. Her ducks were in a nice row.

I didn't know it at the time, but I was showing signs of identity crisis! I knew plenty but was deeply lacking in the revelation department. What I needed was an inside-out kind of Spirit power transformation. Only then would my heart catch up to my head! Only then would I come to understand and know the life, power, and love benefits that come from being a daughter of the Most High God.

The Red Lipstick

I agonized over my situation and compared myself to the neighbor for days. Then God finally spoke through a visual experience I would never forget.

I was taking my morning walk through the neighborhood. It was garbage day, and big black cans lined the street. The garbage trucks had already come through so the lids were open, and I was walking along in deep thought about my circumstances. I was frustrated with my inability to figure things out, and at the same time I was disappointed in myself because I could never get satisfied and be content. At that moment, I was looking intently down at the ground when I came upon what appeared to be an open tube of red lipstick on the sidewalk, someone's discard. Without thinking, I stopped, picked it up, tossed it into the nearest can, and continued on my way. I was in a hurry to get home so I could finish a painting project before picking up the kids from preschool.

My morning became consumed by the project, but in the back of my mind I was still thinking about my friend. Her life versus my life. Her ducks versus my ducks. I just couldn't get past it. Was the whole Christian life just some intellectual game one played with the hope that it would make a difference to God in the end? *There has to be a compelling reason why I am putting myself through all of this,* I kept thinking. *If the Christian life is real, I want to live it. If it's not, what then?*

I was thinking these kinds of thoughts when I went to the kitchen sink to wash my hands, and something really weird caught my eye. *Oh my!* There was a huge red blob on the side of my tennis shoe. *Oh my gosh, it's blood! It's blood on my shoe!* I almost panicked, dabbing at it frantically with a hand towel. *I must be bleeding!*

Suddenly, I made the connection. The red stain was the lipstick I had seen earlier! Somehow it had brushed against the side of my shoe. I understood immediately. God Himself was desperate to tell me something I had nearly forgotten. The climax to the Big Story was true! Because I had believed and received, I was *His*. I was covered by the blood!

The message came in loud and clear: *The provision I made for you through Jesus's shed blood is the difference. You will see!*

I wouldn't understand the full significance of what God said that day until many years later. But at that moment, the blood of Jesus took on a new meaning for me. It was the beginning of a new revelation concerning the power that was mine through Him. My life bore the mark of Jesus's blood, in some strange, supernatural way that I still could not fathom completely. In my heart I believed what He was telling me: even though I was suffering from many disappointments and shattered dreams, Jesus's blood would make all the difference to me in the end. As you may surmise, it most certainly did! More on that in a later chapter.

But for now, let's focus on the Big Story.

The Story of the Blood

Long before Jesus came to Earth, God instituted a temporary system of forgiving sins based on the blood sacrifice of goats and bulls. The faith of the person performing the sacrifice, called the high priest, brought temporary forgiveness to himself and others under his charge when the life of an animal was given in exchange for sins that needed to be forgiven. The blood of the animal had to be applied to a literal covering or lid on the altar called the mercy seat before forgiveness could take full effect. However, this procedure never had the power needed to buy man back from the power of Satan or make his feelings of guilt disappear. Sin was not truly taken away. In fact, the discipline served mainly as a reminder of sinfulness and the need to be forgiven (Hebrews 10:1–4).

The secret climax of the Big Story—the culmination of God's redemption strategy—was that *God was willing to pay the predetermined, supernatural price required both to forgive our sins and to free us from Satan, slave owner and father of lies, once and for all.*

How was the price required for our freedom determined? The answer to that question is mysterious and supernatural and has remained hidden. However, God, in His omniscience, knew precisely the cost from the beginning, before the foundation of the world. He knew the perfect blood of Jesus shed was the price required to set His people free from darkness, fear, death, selfishness, shame, guilt, sin consciousness, and futility. But He kept this information hidden until the time had fully come. Not even Satan knew!

> *God chose him as your ransom long before the world began, but now in these last days he has been revealed for your sake.*
> 1 PETER 1:20

Satan is not omniscient, all-knowing. Before Jesus's blood was shed he was arrogant enough to think he would always have the upper hand as regards our human condition. What was he thinking? He knew God had power to save the world, but that He only worked through people. Who could then set the world free from Satan's slave trade? No one short of God Himself—in human form—could even come close! But if God did come to Earth, Satan mused, He would have to give up the glory of heaven and become subject to the laws of sin and death, just like everyone else who lived under slave rule. Surely He would never choose to live like that!

But God fooled Satan, who had no full understanding, no ability to know of His secret plans and purposes. For since the beginning, Jesus had been with God. And since the beginning, Jesus had planned and agreed to give up His glory in heaven to come to Earth and save the human race. His thoughts and plans did require Him to suffer a great loss. But He was willing to do it. Because He is love. And because He is a giver.

So at just the right time, God secretly sent Jesus, a part of Himself, to Earth—in the form of a helpless baby. And so the groundwork was laid for God to partner with Jesus, a man, born into slavery just like everyone else. Yet He was unlike all others. He was God in the flesh. And His blood was perfect, untainted.

In the beginning the Word already existed. The Word was with God, and the Word was God. He existed in the beginning with God. God created everything through him, and nothing was created except through him.
JOHN 1:1–3

So the Word became human and made his home among us. He was full of unfailing love and faithfulness. And we have seen his glory, the glory of the Father's one and only Son.
JOHN 1:14

You know the story of how it all happened. An angel appeared to Mary, a young and humble virgin. She had found favor with God. And through her, God would reveal to the world His Son, whose name would be Jesus ("the Lord Saves"). Mary agreed to receive into her womb the seed of God through the power of the Holy Spirit. In so doing, she willingly agreed to suffer the ridicule of an illegitimate pregnancy and possible rejection from her betrothed, Joseph, a young carpenter. But an angel had also appeared to Joseph in a dream, and he too believed the Good News, that this Son would save His people from their sins. So Joseph graciously accepted the responsibility that God had given him and took Mary as his wife.

The X Factor

In one of the Big Story's strangest and most awe-inspiring scenes, Jesus was born in a stable in Bethlehem. He grew up like everyone else. He learned to walk and talk. He learned about His Father God in the temple. And He grew up into manhood and faced all the same temptations and problems and issues that everyone else faced.

But the life that poured out of Jesus was entirely unique—a result of that mysterious, hidden identity that He had carried since birth, the origins of which were heavenly, never tainted by the father of lies. Even as a young child, Jesus exhibited those X-Factor qualities that everyone, including Satan, observed—strong, almost indescribable characteristics that suggested greatness, destiny, authority, influence. Satan figured that He should be watched closely. But he could not quite discern what Jesus's exact purpose might be.

The term X-Factor was first used in the 1930s and can be defined as: (1) a variable in a given situation that could have the most significant impact on the outcome. (2) an indescribable quality or something that you cannot put your finger on. (3) a circumstance, quality or person that has a strong but unpredictable influence.

And so Jesus grew up, rose above life's circumstances, and lived the perfect life. His capacity to know and understand God as His Father—and to commune with Him and manifest His Spirit—was without limit. However, Jesus grew up into the fullness of God's plan and purpose around age thirty. At that point, whatever the Father God did and said was what Jesus did and said. It was that simple. And so He walked the earth loving people—preaching the Good News, casting out demons, and healing those with physical, emotional, and spiritual infirmities. All along He knew the time would come when He would perform the ultimate will of God. It was the reason He had come to Earth.

About three years after Jesus's official ministry began, Satan had determined that He was too unpredictable, too likely to cause an undesirable outcome. And so Satan gathered the powers of darkness and planned to kill Jesus on a cross, to put Him down once and for all. But evil could not know the plan and intention of God. God would turn this heinous act into something unimaginable. The surprise climax of the Big Story would finally occur. The tables would turn. God's team would win.

And so God watched His Son being thrashed and beaten and then hung on a cross to die the cruelest of all slow and agonizing deaths. Then, seemingly, it was finished. Jesus was dead. Satan smirked and assumed he had won the fight. But he had no idea what God had just done!

Highly valued, sinless blood had been needed to buy us back from the Evil One. Right under Satan's nose, Jesus's willingness to shed His blood on that cross had started the redemptive process. But God had to do something else so our sin and shame would never again be an issue—so we could know His love and forgiveness, be empowered and purpose-driven and have an intimate relationship with Him once again.

As Jesus hung on the cross, God supernaturally cast all the sin and evil in the world—past, present, and future—onto Jesus's body. Then for the first time ever, God turned His back on His Son, abandoning Him and leaving Him to die all alone. The Father was forced to separate Himself from His sin-laden Son, because He could not have fellowship with evil.

It was the worst thing God could possibly do to a person He loved. Not only was Jesus's physical pain beyond comprehension, but the spiritual, emotional, and psychological pain were equally great. But God had no choice. Justice required that a sinless Someone shed blood and take punishment for our sin so we could be forgiven once and for all. This was also the only way God could get the power of our sin removed so we could then walk free of entanglements and receive the benefits of peace, freedom, and the power of the Holy Spirit!

> *For Christ did not enter into a holy place made with human hands,*
> *which was only a copy of the true one in heaven. He entered*
> *into heaven itself to appear now before God on our behalf. And he*
> *did not enter heaven to offer himself again and again, like the high*
> *priest here on earth who enters the Most Holy Place year after year*
> *with the blood of an animal. If that had been necessary, Christ*
> *would have had to die again and again, ever since the world began.*
> *But now, once for all time, he has appeared at the end of the*
> *age to remove sin by his own death as a sacrifice.*
> HEBREWS 9:24–26

The Good News

The climax to the Big Story happened when Jesus's blood was shed. Through that act, our sins were not only forgiven, but for all who believed and received the Good News of forgiveness, sin was also removed and the power of sin defused! Satan had played right in to God's hand. At the cross, he was sure he had defeated God. But suddenly, he faltered. Had he lost his touch, been crippled? No doubt something very powerful had occurred in the spirit realm! Then he realized what had happened! A veil once separating humans from God had been torn from top to bottom, granting them full access to the power and presence of God the Father!

The door to human restoration had opened! Men could again

have fellowship with God—the same as they had before Adam and Eve ate of the tree! Satan knew he was in trouble.

But that was only the half of it! Three days later, Jesus was resurrected from the dead! God had made a visual statement to the world that could not be ignored. The resurrection proved that Jesus's shed blood had overcome sin and death, creating a way for us to be restored to our original identity as sons and daughters.

It was the most important act of God in human history. But to get to that point, God had to work through people! Even Jesus partnered with God while on Earth, just like the rest of us—though He was the only person to do it perfectly. And since the Big Story is not yet over, God continues to partner with those of us who are willing to participate!

Since Jesus was God and man at the same time, does this mean God the Father partnered with Himself? Yes! God's plan was to dwell among us—both to save us from Satan's slave trade and to demonstrate the how-tos of partnership with God the Father. We are not perfect partners, as Jesus was. But when we follow His example, we come much closer! Do you have an expectation that God will do something extraordinary as a result of your faith and partnership? If yes, what? What must you do to get started?

Obviously, we have advantages in this partnership process that pre-resurrection humanity did not have. God defeated Satan once and for all on the cross. As a result, we have the ability to manifest God's love and power. And we have Jesus's example of how it can be done and are equipped to follow His lead through the power of the Holy Spirit.

Since the cross, God's partnership objective has been to bring heaven to Earth through His people, simultaneously destroying the works of the devil, for the Evil One is still active and at work in the world and in the affairs of men. But he has suffered a huge setback! We can be released from his grip when we apply the Spirit power that comes from Jesus's perfect blood. We can declare him powerless in our lives! We can show others how to do the same. The process of redemption repeats itself over and over again through us as we touch others with the Spirit, one person at a time!

Today, my friend, turn to the Giver of all good things. Believe His Good News! Accept His gifts—relationship, forgiveness, wholeness, and life through the power of the Holy Spirit. Agree to partnership with Him. Use what faith you have now to apply Jesus's blood to your life and circumstances. Granted, it is a mystery how or why this works. But the Bible is clear. There is amazing power in Jesus's blood shed for us. It is the single greatest reason we can receive everything we need.

He is so rich in kindness and grace that he purchased our
freedom with the blood of his Son and forgave our sins.
EPHESIANS 1:7

And this same God who takes care of me will supply all your needs
from his glorious riches, which have been given to us in Christ Jesus.
PHILIPPIANS 4:19

Say it out loud! "Lord, I trust You! You are giving me everything I need!"

Discussion Questions

Look up the Scriptures listed and reflect on the questions presented. Possible "answers", along with Scripture references from the New Living Translation, can be located at the back of this book.

1. Jesus's mother was a virgin, and His Father was God. (Isaiah 7:14;

Matthew 1:23) Mary provided the egg. God created "something from nothing" and provided the seed—which created blood, and consequently, the life of Jesus. Life is in the blood. (Leviticus 17:11) Logically speaking, what is the constitution of Jesus's blood and life?

2. Before Jesus came, redemption was the price that had to be paid to free a slave. (Leviticus 25:47–54) What did the shedding of Jesus's perfect, sinless blood accomplish for us? (Ephesians 1:7; Hebrews 9:12; Hebrews 2:16–17; Hebrews 9:26; Isaiah 43:25)

3. To receive this forgiveness and redemption from God, what must we do? (Romans 10:9–10)

4. Believing means applying faith. What is faith? (Hebrews 11:1) How do we get faith? (Romans 10:17)

5. What happens when we have faith? (John 1:12–13; John 3:1–8; Ezekiel 36:26–27; John 14:6–7; Romans 5:18; Luke 17:5–6; Mark 9:23–25)

Personal Reflections

1. As was true for Abraham, God has not lost sight of His goal for your life. What do you think He has in mind for you? What foibles must He work around? Are you willing to let Him work with you on it? What are your deepest needs? Can you depend on this God of all gods to meet them?

2. If you have already believed and received the Good News about Jesus's blood, your sin has been removed, and you have been rescued from the grip of Satan's power. Do you sense that this is true? If so, how does this knowledge make you feel? If you don't sense this truth, what might the problem be?

3. Jesus grew up into a full understanding of His created destiny as God's Son. Likewise, will you grow up in your understanding of what it means to be a son or daughter of the Most High God and discover your created destiny? As a result, will you rise high above your circumstances? Will you commune with your Father God and manifest His Spirit in increasing measures? Can you give examples of how this might be happening already?

CHAPTER 4

RELEASE

For the Kingdom of God is not just a lot of talk;
it is living by God's Power.
1 CORINTHIANS 4:20

Key #4: God has made available to His children all the power needed to live the life of abundance He has promised. However, we must overcome nearsightedness, stubbornness, and hardheartedness through the RELEASE of bondages that keep us enslaved and unable to embrace our new way of life.

ELECTRICITY IS EVERYWHERE. We can't literally see it. But we know it's there—not just because we've been told that it exists, but because we experience what it can do for us every day. As a result, if the power goes out in our homes, there's no fear. We don't like the inconvenience, but we know it's just a matter of time before the power will turn back on. And we will do whatever is necessary to get the power we need. We will walk all over an airport to find an available outlet so our phone's battery can charge for a while, right?

Likewise, the supernatural power of God's presence is everywhere—and God intends for us to harness that power and use it to destroy the work of Satan and expand the kingdom of God!

Remember, we were made to be like God. That's why Jesus shed His blood—not only to remove our sin, but to open a floodgate of God's Spirit to the earth so that we can now follow in His footsteps and do the things He did, and even greater!

On top of all this, Jesus showed us how to do it! He lived in God's Presence. That's how He knew God's heart. That's where He got the revelation He needed. So He could appropriate faith and release power. That is how He healed the sick, cast out demons, effectively preached the Good News, and ministered to the broken-hearted. Granted, He was God in the flesh. But He was also fully man. He is our model.

Jesus did not come to bring us another religion! He came to shed perfect blood that would release the power of the kingdom! The Greek word for "power" in many New Testament verses, including 1 Corinthians 4:20, is dunamis, which means "miraculous power, strength, ability, force" and is the root word for dynamite, dynamo, and dynamic. The resurrection proved that this degree of power had been released and made available to anyone who will receive it. Christianity is set apart from other religions, which have no blood, no resurrection, and consequently, no "dunamis."

The Power Package

Because such great power has been provided, we must learn to utilize faith to get it. We must go where God is. Hang out in His presence. Get charged. Then we can expect His power and love to flow through us. God can use us to perform the impossible!

But we have to start at the beginning. Only a small amount of faith is required to get started. This is where God has pricked our hearts in some way, through a nudge or a revelation or visual experience, and in that place God shows us His heart. He loves us! He has been pursuing us! So we turn and follow His unconditional love. We are entering into His presence!

Then we recognize another gift, the Holy Spirit, the power of God born in us. All things are new! God has given us a vision of life that far surpasses anything we have known. And we are trusting Him. We are not focusing on what we literally see. Rather, we are focused on the vision He gives us. And as we press into His presence, He increases our understanding about many things. We sense that our sin has been removed. And there is a Spirit fire in our hearts. And it is burning away bondages that have kept us enslaved and limited for a very long time—maybe even a lifetime.

"Forget the former things; do not dwell on the past."
ISAIAH 43:18

The Release from Bondage

God desires that we live in peace, freedom, and power! And why wouldn't we want that kind of life for ourselves? But the sad truth is that we don't always cooperate with His plans for us. Many times we have spent decades—or longer—living apart from God's presence. By default we have served a counterfeit father—the slave master, Satan—who has taught us lies, propped up our false identities, and kept us in bondage. Even after we turn and follow our true Father, we don't cut ties completely to our old lives due to lack of revelation and/or disobedience. We are not easily disentangled from our past!

There is a visual story in the Bible that portrays Abraham's children caught in bondage and then released, but not able to embrace the new life given due to nearsightedness, stubbornness, and hardheartedness. The story implies that God has done His part to free us. He has already given us everything we need. Now we must do our part. We must receive the vision He has for us, then walk in faith and obedience. Otherwise, we will not experience the release of Spirit power within us!

There are three meanings of RELEASE in this book, all of them equally important to understand and apply on your journey to freedom. First, God has already done what was required to get us humans (1) RELEASED from bondage to Satan through Jesus's death and resurrection. The Big Story account explaining how God freed Abraham's lineage from slavery in Egypt is a symbolic example of such release. However, in this same example, even after the slaves were technically freed, they continued to live in mental and emotional bondage to their present and past circumstances. God could not send His people into the Promised Land until they (2) RELEASED all soulish attachments and embraced the future He had planned for them. Likewise, when we are able to trust the provision God has made for us in Jesus, thereby releasing our mental and emotional hang-ups, (3) the Spirit power in us is fully RELEASED and we move quickly toward the power-filled life of peace and freedom that God has planned for us.

Abraham's descendants had been enslaved in Egypt for four hundred years. Remember, God had previously promised to give these people a spacious and desirable land. Now He was ready to fulfill His promise. But first the people had to be set free. So Moses, a descendant of Abraham, was the human God picked to get these two million plus people released and settled in their new land.

God spoke to Moses from a burning bush and told him what to do. *Go to Egypt. Speak to the ruler of the land, the pharaoh, and tell him what I demand. Perform miracles so the children of Abraham will believe and cooperate with the plan.*

Moses did as he was told, and the people believed because of the miracles God had equipped Moses to perform. The pharaoh was not so easily convinced. So God told Moses to tell the people this: they were to apply the blood of a lamb to the doorjamb of every household. When they did, an Angel of Death passed over every house where the blood had been applied. The Egyptian households were not covered by the blood. Consequently, the firstborn of all their households was slain. Finally, Pharaoh let the people go!

What an event! God's presence—in the form of a cloud by day and a pillar of fire by night—led them. The exodus came off without a hitch! When the former slaves got to the Red Sea, Moses raised his staff and the waters parted. God had made a way for them to cross on dry land, with a giant wall of water on either side! The Pharaoh had since changed his mind about their release, so the Egyptian army was in hot pursuit! But when they nearly caught up to God's people and attempted to cross from behind, the waters crashed in on them—in the nick of time!

> Then the LORD said to Moses, "Why are you crying out to me? Tell the people to get moving! Pick up your staff and raise your hand over the sea! Divide the water so the Israelites can walk through the middle of the sea on dry ground."
> EXODUS 14:15–16

God put Moses in charge. He told him exactly what to do. Then He expected him to do it! He had given Moses authority.

The first victory had been won! Celebration was in order. However, desert circumstances were less than ideal. And much of the people's time was spent bickering and questioning Moses's judgment on daily provisions. In actuality, God had miraculously supplied all they needed—nothing fancy, but adequate! Clearly Moses's leadership was more than adequate. And the visual evidence of God's presence and protection was constant.

But the people were stiff-necked, disagreeable, and ungrateful. They even wished they were still in Egypt. Imagine that! They wished for a return to slavery rather than face the challenges of freedom!

In light of all the miracles performed, how could the people so quickly lose sight of the promise God had given—a new life of prosperity and freedom in a land "flowing with milk and honey"? Granted, the journey to the land would not be easy. But God had gone before them so far, He had been behind them all the way, and His hand was on their heads! If they would relax and submit to God's plans, the time would pass quickly. The days of transition and preparation for new life would be completed sooner rather than later!

For us too, there is a bridge between the old life and the new life, between the life of slavery and the life of freedom. The length of time it takes to cross that bridge correlates with the amount of time it takes for our souls—our minds, our wills, and our emotions—to be set free. For this soul area is where we get caught up—where we get stuck, attached, bound, enslaved. But God has a plan for us! If we submit to the plan, the transition period will pass quickly. We will get to where He is leading us much faster. Submit! God is with you on the journey into your new life. He knows where you have been. He knows where He is taking you.

> *Since you have heard about Jesus and have learned the truth that comes from him, throw off your old sinful nature and your former way of life, which is corrupted by lust and deception. Instead, let the Spirit renew your thoughts and attitudes. Put on your new nature, created to be like God—truly righteous and holy.*
> EPHESIANS 4:21–24

The Wilderness Journey Extended

For the Israelites, the rebellion continued while Moses climbed a mountain to commune with God and receive His holy laws for living. It took forty days. So the people moaned and groaned and even threw a huge party, indulging in feasting and drinking and pagan revelry. The tipping point occurred when they gathered up all the gold they could find, melted it in the fire, and cast a statue of a golden calf—an idol!

Finally, Moses delivered and explained the holy laws. A degree of punishment was dealt to the people for their deliberate acts of rebellion. Then they camped at the border of the Promised Land, where the presence of God had settled.

It should have been an eleven-day trek from that spot to the place in the land they would occupy. But first, a delegation of spies was sent to survey the land and its people. Alas! When the spies returned, ten of the twelve gave a bad report. "We can't take this land. The people are too big. They are way stronger than us." Upon receipt of this news, the people grumbled and wept even more.

Again, God forgave. But this time, the nation's disobedience and unbelief would cost them something—time. God's decree dictated they wander in the wilderness for forty more years. Moses told the people to turn around and head back to the desert.

"But no!" they wailed. "We have made a mistake!" They insisted on going through with the plan to enter. An army of "warriors" blundered their way into the land, without Moses's blessing and without the presence of God. Immediately, the occupants of the land thwarted the attempt and drove them back into the desert, fearing for their lives!

Leading with the Soul

To review, God made us with three distinct parts—spirit, soul, and body. Our attachments, or bondages, are generally created at the soul level and can be represented by a dominance of "thinking" or "feeling." Hence there are two types of people, the "thinkers" and the "feelers." Some people operate equally in both styles. But most people are dominant in one or the other. The people who sent the delegation of spies, analyzed the data, and decided not to enter the land were thinkers. The people who moaned and groaned, threw a rebellious party, and made an idol were the feelers! They were also the ones in charge of blundering their way onto the land without God's blessing.

Are you in bondage to your thinking? Do you overanalyze everything? Do you plot and plan and make decisions based on your intellect? Do you have a hard time sleeping at night because you cannot shut off your mind? Do you have a hard time going into the presence of God and just receiving from Him—because you are thinking your own thoughts, making your own plans? Thinkers are controllers. They have a hard time expressing feelings. They are doers. Their greatest fear is not having control. Therefore, their greatest "need" is to maintain control.

Are you in bondage to your feelings? Feelers whine and cry when they don't get their way. They act without thinking because their feelings—which can come on suddenly—are controlling them. They cannot let go of things, because they are emotionally attached. They suck life and love out of other people because they are trying to get their own emotional needs met. They stay in bad relationships. They can't be alone. They can't think logically about decisions because their minds are clouded by emotions. They are easily overwhelmed. They are burdened. They have a hard time sleeping at night because they live in fear of not getting their needs met. They "need" support.

To become free, we must release our bondages (i.e. no longer allow our soulish minds or emotions to lead). Learning to rest in the secret place of God's presence, where there is an interaction of our faith with God's Spirit, brings about a release of power in us that sets us free from these things that have enslaved us.

The One Thing

God's decision to send the Israelites back to the desert was final. His hands were tied! Remember, the Spirit of God simply will not move except through faith and obedience.

Eventually, the people did miraculously and effortlessly take possession of the land. God would never renege on a promise. But it did take forty years for the unbelieving, disobedient generation to die off before the next generation could embrace the vision and fulfill the promise God had made.

Obviously, God's intention was to bless these people! But somehow the message was not getting through. Collectively, they had no eyes to see or ears to hear. Consequently, there was no faith. And without faith, there is no power. And with no power, there is no capability to do the right thing.

If only God's children had not held so tightly to the One Thing— the thing that was holding them back from receiving the power and ultimate blessing. In their case, the One Thing was *the past.*

There is always One Thing. My One Thing is probably different from yours! But regardless, the One Thing is keeping us from attaining the next level of God's presence. Sometimes we can't even see what it is! But God knows. And He will show us what it is when we ask Him. Dear friend, your One Thing must be released. Any thing, person, or situation that keeps you focused on yourself is the One Thing. *Release* it today!

Take the rich young ruler as an example (Mark 10:17–22). When he came to Jesus, he had been sidetracked to the extent that he hadn't even taken the first real step into God's presence. Oh, he was religious all right! He plainly stated that he had worked very hard to keep the holy laws for living. And he had been quite successful in that endeavor, according to the story. But he knew there was something missing. Something that was keeping him pinned down and unable to receive the salvation about which Jesus was preaching. He just couldn't put his finger on what that One Thing was exactly.

But Jesus knew. And He told him, point-blank. "Your riches. That's the One Thing that is keeping you from seeing the truth. Go and sell all you have and give it to the poor. Then you will be free from the bondage that is holding you back." The young man walked away very sad because he was not willing to relinquish the One Thing that would set his spirit free.

At the point of salvation, or rebirth, our spirits are literally "set free" from prison. Then our spirit is joined to the Spirit of God. "But the person who is joined to the Lord is one spirit with him" (1 Corinthians 6:17). After rebirth, our souls (mind, will, and emotions) must be set free through the regenerative work of the Holy Spirit. Typically, our One Thing is linked to a bondage we are holding onto at the soul level. Thinkers process things differently than feelers. But whether the One Thing is related to a thinking bondage (mind) or a feeling bondage (emotions)—or both—the problem must be released.

When we apply Jesus's blood to our mind, will, and emotions, we are free to share Jesus's mind and heart—to see our life and the lives of others the way He does. Our emotions are not all out of whack. Our minds are not cluttered with unneeded minutiae. Like Jesus, we can release to the Father all concerns. Like Him, we have no fear of the future, because we receive from our Father God all that we need. And we have no concern for the past. Our sins are no more. We are washed clean. There is no guilt and no condemnation. We are free to live life in perfect balance, according to His perfect will and purpose!

The First Steps to Release

I shared previously that my One Thing was my desire for a mutually enjoyable, respectful, and intimate relationship with a man. This is not necessarily a bad thing! But my desire for a compatible mate had such a grip on me that I would repeatedly make poor decisions based on that preoccupation. These mistakes consistently caused me to fall short of the presence of God and the power of the Holy Spirit.

God's hands were tied, because I was not allowing Him to work in my life in such a way that His power could manifest.

But I thank God for the revelation He finally gave me! Granted, I had to fall flat on my face to get it. But at that point he had my attention!

First, God allowed me to see clearly the bondage under which I had been living for most of my life. Then He showed me the steps I needed to take. He said, "Get the steps right, and the power of the Holy Spirit will manifest!" Each step is a key, unlocking the way into a transformed life lived in the presence of God.

I've already laid out the initial steps He showed me in these first four chapters. But here are the highlights for review:

Step 1: REALIZE what God is saying to you. Ask Him to give you a clear revelation. He has already been nudging you; otherwise you wouldn't be reading this book! Go to a place where you can listen. When you think you hear something, write it down so you won't forget. Or just be aware that God may speak at any time. Pay attention! Keep a notepad beside your bed. Many of my realizations come in dreams or in sudden thought after I wake.

Step 2: REROUTE! Consistently run toward God, not away from Him. This means to always keep the need to be with Him, in His presence, your main focus. Certainly, the very first time we enter into His presence is the point of our salvation. But that is just the beginning! We must learn to "go" there to Him time and time again. A quiet, private place where you are likely not to be disturbed or distracted is ideal to find this "secret place." It can be a bedroom or a beach. No doubt you will view this as a sacrifice. However, the more time you spend moving toward God when no one else is watching, the more of Him you will see and know. Eventually, you will view this time spent as an invaluable part of your human existence. Eventually, you will learn to "go" there and even "live" there no matter your surroundings!

Step 3: RECEIVE the power and forgiveness that comes from Jesus's blood shed for you. And receive everything else you need!

God knows what we need better than we do. So receive His presence, along with all the other things He has in mind for you—every day! Affirm it out loud. "Lord, I receive the power and revelation of the Holy Spirit! I trust You! You are giving me everything I need!"

Step 4: If you need to, RELEASE to Him the One Thing. This will magnify the release of the Holy Spirit already at work in you. Remember, you are not alone in this struggle. God's Spirit is your Helper. He knows what your One Thing is and how to help you release it. Press in to His Spirit! Then wait until He shows you what comes next. It will likely involve a sudden release of more power in you that magnifies all the other steps and continues to build momentum.

Thy Kingdom Come, Thy Will Be Done

God has done His part. He sent Jesus so we could once again be His children and receive the Holy Spirit's power. Now that we have the power, He wants us to do our part. Remember, He only works through people! So we have to use our faith to serve His purposes. That's how His Spirit gets placed in us in the first place: through our faith. Then His power can be magnified and released. It flows through us! And when His Power is RELEASED, the work of Satan is destroyed and the kingdom of God on Earth is increased, not just in us, but in others through us. This is the plan God had from the beginning. His power and love can be transferred to anyone we touch.

So, my friend, if you still don't have faith that God exists, or that He loves you, or that He would desire to see you made whole, let me reach out and touch you with my faith. I wrote this book in part for the purpose of touching you with the power of God in me, which burst into flame so many, many years ago—a power that grew and then faded, but which is being fanned back into flame through the RELEASE of the Holy Spirit. It is increasing in me even now!

God sent Jesus to the earth to manifest God's presence, to shed valuable blood, to die and to rise again so the power of evil could be destroyed. And all of this was accomplished, my friend, so I could go into His presence, receive His power, and eventually touch you! Now faith is growing and increasing in you too, possibly for the first time. You too have become a conduit of His Spirit and its power. You are coming into His presence. Darkness is being removed. Now there is only light. And He is breathing more and more power into you. You are receiving His touch. You are being healed emotionally, spiritually, and physically. And now you too can go and touch others!

Praise God! We have reclaimed our true identity as God's children! He is living His life in and through us. And by the power of the blood—and through our life stories and our willingness to give and be a touch to others—we are moving deeper and deeper into His presence.

When the spirit is not healed, the soul and body suffer. When the soul is not healed, the body will suffer. Here is a healing prayer for you:

"Father God, I take the blood of Jesus, and I apply it to my spirit. My spirit is now free! I have been born again into Your kingdom, where there are no limits! Living in Your kingdom allows me to receive all that I need for fullness, healing, and power.

"Now, I apply the blood of Jesus to my mind. Specifically, I apply it to the problem concerning _____. I am no longer in bondage to my mind. Instead, I am free to rest in Your thoughts about all situations. It is my privilege to rest in Your creativity and Your perspective, along with all Your plans and ideas for my participation in the Big Story. My productivity is increasing, because You are in control of my mind! The topper: I am becoming more emotionally expressive!

"I apply the blood of Jesus to my emotions. Specifically,
I apply it to the problem concerning _____.
I am no longer in bondage to my emotions. Instead, I rest,
assured. I see people the way You do. I focus on the things that
You are most burdened about (versus my own personal burdens).
But I am never consumed or overwhelmed by any burden, because
I filter all people and situations through Your eyes. I am no
longer overly sensitive and easily offended. It's not about me!
I have released everything that keeps me focused on myself.
Instead, I have Your intuition. And I express Your love
and compassion. The Holy Spirit controls my emotions.
The topper: I am becoming more productive.
"I apply the blood of Jesus to my will. Thank you, Lord! My
will is now in alignment with Your perfect will and purpose.
My mind, will, and emotions are free! I am free to release control,
fear, and guilt. I am no longer in bondage to the One Thing!

"I also apply the blood of Jesus to my body. The power
of the Holy Spirit is literally flowing through the cells in
my body now. I am healed in my spirit, my soul, and my body!
Sickness and disease are being healed and removed, in Jesus's
name. Thank you, Lord, for the provision you have given
of Jesus's blood and the life-giving Spirit that is mine as a result.
Thank you, Lord! You give me everything I need!"

Discussion Questions

Look up the Scriptures listed and reflect on the questions presented. Possible "answers", along with Scripture references from the New Living Translation, can be located at the back of this book.

1. After Jesus's blood was shed, what happened to signify that people had gained access to God's presence and power? (Mark 15:37–38; Matthew 27:45, 50–53)

2. After Jesus rose from the dead, He went straight to the Father to apply His sinless blood to the heavenly mercy seat. (John 20:11–18; Hebrews 9:11–12) What do you think this accomplished?

3. After Jesus's blood was applied, He appeared to His disciples. What did He do and say to them? (John 20:22) In another account, Jesus told them to expect something at a later date—something greater! What was that? (Luke 24:49)

4. Where is Jesus now? What is He doing for us there? (Hebrews 8:1–2; Hebrews 7:25; Acts 2:33)

5. If the same Spirit that raised Jesus from the dead lives in us, what kind of life should we expect to live? (2 Corinthians 4:7; 2 Corinthians 12:9; Ephesians 3:20–21; 2 Timothy 1:7)

6. The "Power Package" is this: we can manifest God's selfless, unconditional love because we are made in His image. We have His DNA—Divine Nature Ability! How do we move past a toxic, selfish, prideful kind of "love" to God's pure, selfless, unconditional love? (Matthew 22:36–40; John 13:34; John 14:21; 1 Timothy 1:5; Romans 5:5; Ephesians 3:17)

7. God cannot work or provide Spirit power except through our faith and obedience. Even Jesus had to apply faith and obedience to finish the assignment He had been given on Earth. (Philippians 2:8) Where does our faith and obedience come from? (Philippians 2:13)

8. At the point of spiritual rebirth, our spirit is joined to God's Spirit. (1 Corinthians 6:17) Is it God's Spirit joined to ours that triggers faith? Or does our initial faith trigger the entrance of His Spirit?

Personal Reflections

1. Has your One Thing prevented you from entering into relationship with God? Or if you have received salvation, has the One Thing encumbered or distracted you in such a way that life has taken over and you have found yourself powerless to rise above circumstances? How has the One Thing impeded your progress?

2. The Spirit power gives us new eyes and a new vision. What do you "see"? Do you still see bondages of your mind or emotions? Is your One Thing associated with one of these bondages? What progress are you making in terms of releasing this Thing that is holding you back and restricting your vision?

CHAPTER 5:
_____

RENEW

"Your mistake is that you don't know the Scriptures,
and you don't know the power of God."
MATTHEW 22:29

Key #5: Power flow occurs when we receive the same deep revelations that Jesus received, from the same sources Jesus tapped: the Word of God and the presence of God. We must follow the same recipe Jesus followed, starting with faith, then applying the Word and the presence in equal measures. The result is a RENEWED mind and a changed heart—a transformed life filled with peace, freedom and power.

IF WE ARE TO WALK AS JESUS WALKED, we must first think as He thought. Only then can we see people as He saw them, love them as He loved them, and minister to them as He did, through genuine love and compassion and with miraculous signs and wonders. Remember, His desire is that we do even greater things than He did. Through us His peace, freedom, and power will change the world—one person at a time!

But how do we get there? Perhaps we have already believed and received the Good News. God's Spirit power has been born in us. But we have become sidelined or sidetracked, wandering without purpose. Regardless of the reason, our journey into the Promised Land has been extended. And so we sit on the periphery, waiting. We so want to enter the land! We want to live the kind of life that we know God promised us. But our circumstances are still defining us and holding us back. God forbid we get sent back to the wilderness! We do not want more aimless wandering!

Remember, we can't enter the land—or go to the next level—without the revelation God is trying to give us. And perhaps that revelation has been hidden—until now! Yes, that which has been hidden is being revealed. The domino effect leads to new thought processes that change our hearts. Our new hearts change our demeanor and our words and our actions. Our lives are being transformed!

But this is just the beginning. God is forever in a mode of showing us new things! He never stops! There is always a greater revelation of truth that allows us to experience more and more freedom and power. Perhaps the more we "see and hear," the more we can participate in what God is already doing all around us and in the world at large.

This kind of transformation happens in very practical ways as we learn to hear the voice of God. I was once a on a two-and-a-half-hour flight to Dallas. I was sitting next to a young African American man. We never spoke or even made eye contact. I did notice that he mostly slept. He also had on earphones the entire flight. I slept some and spent the rest of the time reading a book called *Approaching the Heart of Prophecy* by Graham Cooke.

While reading, I thought about how God wanted to give me His thoughts so I could see others the way He sees them and have the same burdens for them that He has. Near the end of the flight, I closed the book. At landing, I looked over at this guy, still sleeping—with his mouth open! Ha! He appeared to be about thirty-five years old. Immediately, my thought was, *Aww, he's someone's son.* Then my thoughts took an unexpected turn: *He is his mother's son!* Then this: *God is holding his mother in the palm of His hand.*

The Half & Half

Back to the issue: the words and actions that came out of Jesus's life were rooted in the revelation He received from two sources: the Scriptures and the power of God. I think of this as the "half & half." If there had been no half & half in His life, surely there would have been no power flow. Yes, Jesus was the visible representation of the invisible God. But He was still fully man. And even though His heart was never tainted by sin, He still had to grow up into the revelation of who He was and what His purpose was here on earth. Jesus required this revelation to get the power flowing.

So through obedience, even at a very early age, Jesus exercised faith. This means He consciously used and applied faith by bringing it out in the open—i.e. He did not keep it to Himself or allow it to remain hidden. Then, in equal measures, over and over again, He meditated on the Scriptures and applied God's Spirit and presence. This continuous practice resulted in an ever-increasing revelation of truth.

To follow in His steps, we need the same kind of revelation. However, our hearts and our minds—unlike His—are tainted at birth. And our spirits are dead until we reroute for the first time and receive salvation. Then God's Spirit activates within us, and we begin our journey to heaven. But to get the revelation we need to manifest God's power and rise above our circumstances in this earthly life, we have to—through obedience—follow the same recipe Jesus followed! Only then can we come even close to walking as He did—destroying the work of the Evil One and transferring peace, freedom, and power to others!

Recipe for Peace, Freedom, and Power
(or Walking as Jesus Did)

Ingredients:

(1) Faith, obtained through hearing the Word of God

(2) The Word of God, written or spoken

(3) The Holy Spirit's power, found in His presence

Steps:

(1) Start with faith, any amount.

(2) Apply equal parts Word of God and Spirit power.

(3) Mix thoroughly and repeatedly until truth forms.

(4) Set aside and wait until revelation rises to the top.

(5) Skim. Then use to speak God's purposes and remove Satan's lies.

(6) Give away a generous portion to ensure unlimited supply.

(7) Keep reapplying Word of God and Spirit power until power flows.

(8) Repeat.

Result: A renewed mind and a changed heart—peace, freedom, and power.

Yield: Unlimited.

Hint: Continued applications of Word of God and Spirit power increase faith.

Increased faith builds momentum and magnifies results.

We must follow this recipe to a T. We cannot alter the ingredients, and we cannot change up the measures! The half & half is critical. We must meditate on the Scriptures and spend equal time in the presence of the Holy Spirit—seeking the truth about who we are as God's children and listening to His voice. Over time, the Spirit illuminates the written Word of God and calls forth other Spirit power manifestations, such as words of knowledge and physical and/or emotional healings. The combination of all these things radically changes our minds about who we are. As a result, we develop a true sense of our purpose on Earth and how we are to go about accomplishing it.

With constant applications, our minds are forever in a state of renewal. But that's not all! Mind renewal also transforms our hearts. This inside-out change effortlessly affects our actions and speech too. And the power of God within us flows out to others in increasing measures. Almost by accident, we walk more and more like Jesus did! We grow up into our true identity as God's children—the identity He has intended for us since the beginning of time!

On the landing strip at the Dallas Airport, the next thought that dominated my mind was this: *Tell the guy what God said about his mother!* The young man was waking up. I could see him out of the corner of my eye. But what was I to do? Nudge him with my elbow? No way! How was I going to give a message like this to someone who still had not looked at me even one time—and who still had earphones wrapped around his head? Understand, this had never happened to me before. I was a bit unsettled. I cried for help: *Father, if You want me to say something, You have got to make this obvious.*

The passengers in front of us were standing to leave. I was in the aisle seat, so I stood first and then inched my way forward into the aisle. I sensed the young man was right behind me. I thought about abruptly turning to tell him. But then I said, *Lord, I just can't do that! Too awkward. But if I bump into him out there somewhere, I promise I will do it!*

I walked as fast as I could off the plane and into the main area, feeling a bit guilty but intent on finding my way to another terminal for the next flight to Houston.

The Truth About Our Counterfeit Father

Why is it such a struggle sometimes for us to receive the mind of Christ? It's because the truth about our spiritual fathers has been hidden. If we can capture the truth about our fathers, we can escape lies and find freedom! But we are born into the lie, where our counterfeit father, Satan, has been our teacher. So even as believers and receivers, our minds are often locked up into his selfish way of thinking. We live as takers, as we were taught. And we are deceived. We don't realize at a deep level that we are Spirit people, loved first by God and bearing His image—made to manifest His love, to be love. So instead, we try to find love and take love. We need love, so we try to extract it from other people. And when we don't get what we need from them, we fall into all sorts of problems, which lead to addictions and bondages and strongholds that keep us frustrated and down. Our hearts flow with selfish "love," unforgiveness, bitterness, fear, isolation, depression, pride, distrust, anxiety, lust, self-sufficiency, self-indulgence, and idolatry, among other characteristics of our counterfeit father.

To transform, we need deep revelation about the nature of our real Father and our relationship to Him. To get that, we must start with faith, which comes from hearing words of truth. But our counterfeit father is a thief who also seeks to kill and destroy us. So his main objective is to steal the word we hear before it penetrates deep into our hearts and produces revelation.

There are three groups of people whose hearts cannot receive the full revelation of our True Father God:

Group 1: The Hardhearted. Satan promotes hardheartedness by keeping people focused on and consumed by current or past circumstances, arousing a range of feelings that continuously grip and dominate their souls. These may include a sense of entitlement, bitterness, mistrust, arrogance, and rebellion. Consequently, the typical response to God's overtures is "I don't want it" and/or "I don't need it."

Sometimes the response among people in this group is "I don't deserve it"—guilt and self-condemnation can also be attributes of a hard heart. Regardless, unresolved brokenness keeps the hardhearted from receiving revelation about forgiveness, relationship, healing, and wholeness. No revelation will occur until the heart is soft and penetrable.

Group 2: The Halfhearted. Sometimes people receive God's words with joy and enthusiasm. But alas, the belief is shallow and develops no root. God says salvation is a free gift that cannot be earned. The halfhearted respond, "I'll take it!" But the halfhearted are simply too busy and distracted to go deeper in their revelation of the Father God. They are half in, half out. They pick up words and look at them, then put them back down. And they don't pay attention! Satan is stealing the words! Then they become generally disinterested. They are either hanging onto salvation by a thread, or they have been deceived into thinking they have received it in the first place. They are an easy target for Satan, who can and does easily steal words left on a heart's surface. Only Words hidden deep within a heart produce true revelation and cannot be removed.

Group 3: The Wholehearted. Among this third group of people, some of God's words have sunk deep down into the heart where Satan cannot touch them—for many of these people are conscientious and serious and give their faith an all-out effort. They spend a lot of time studying the Bible and are very familiar with God's words. And so a degree of revelation has occurred. Certainly, these wholehearted ones understand and receive the basic tenets of salvation and forgiveness. They are on the way to heaven! But here's the rub: in this group much self-effort can be involved. Therefore, the counterfeit father can and does twist what is received. Their head knowledge is moderate to great, but true revelations for this group are infrequent and limited. In other words, information is collected, but there is no deciphering of truth that will radically transform. And head knowledge promotes pride and arrogance! At the same time, sin consciousness produces frustration. Self-generated energy causes weariness. Circumstances define life.

My personal belief is that a lot of well meaning Christians fall into the wholehearted category. I know this is true because I lived in this state myself for decades. From personal experience I know that wholehearted Christians can remain enslaved to the One Thing, a personal idol. Perhaps Satan has tricked them into thinking they cannot live without it. Or maybe they don't know they are enslaved. They are deceived. But they do know *something* is wrong, because they are never able to measure up to God's standards. There is always something they have "done" against God or "not done" for Him, as the case may be. They try to correct these problems but fail time and time again. Then they give up—and never get transformed by the half & half! God's words don't become illumined in their hearts because they are not following the recipe. They are not spending enough time in God's presence, listening to His voice.

Satan is delighted by these mistakes. At this point he can't keep the wholehearted from going to heaven, but he keeps them ineffective and unproductive at bringing heaven back to Earth!

The Truth About Me and My Father God

This is the truth: to receive full revelation about our Father God, we need another kind of heart altogether. A wholehearted *human* effort is not good enough. We need God's heart! We must become *softhearted* like Him.

God's soft heart is within reach. But this is the reality: all too often the wholehearted fall prey to their circumstances and *lose heart altogether*—which is what happened to me.

As mentioned, I was wholehearted for quite a long time. I then backtracked and floundered around in hardheartedness. I stayed in that place for another long while before I was able to exchange my hard heart for a soft one!

I've already explained part of my story. How I followed God at age nineteen. How I worked hard to learn a lot about the Bible and about Him. How I wanted to be a great Christian and experience the deep things. And be married to a strong Christian man. And raise a family in the ways of God. And make a difference. And have a perfect life!

Somewhere along the line I became very frustrated that my circumstances were not turning out like I had anticipated! As I am writing this sentence, I realize that I do not need to point any fingers and place any blame at this stage of the game. I am sincerely way beyond all of that. But I must admit that I allowed myself to be very unhappy for a very long time, and that most of my anguish revolved around my relationship with my husband.

My husband and I met in high school and dated off and on for seven years prior to marriage. He idolized me. I loved that about him. I broke up with him once or twice, and he was nearly devastated over it. I only dated a few people other than him and for no considerable length of time. I liked having a boyfriend at all times—one I could count on. I did not enjoy the uncertainty of being single. He was a person I knew well and trusted and with whom I felt comfortable. He was smart and confident and capable. And after college, marriage seemed to be the obvious step.

I went into it with no hesitation, feeling certain that he would take care of me financially, always idolize me, and give me everything I needed, especially emotional support. He was growing spiritually too, so I figured he would assume the responsibility of spiritual leader of the family as well.

I was set up for a disaster. Until marriage, I had been given everything I ever wanted in the relationship. So when my husband stopped meeting all of my expectations, I didn't know what to think. I didn't know how to react. I was certain that if only he knew God better, my life would surely be happier. If he knew God better, he would love me more, and he would better understand me. He wouldn't be so demanding. He wouldn't make me feel so inadequate. And he would spend more time helping me discipline the kids. God would bless his business, and we would have more money. Things wouldn't be so tough.

Never mind that knowing God better would have given him a more satisfying, peaceful, Spirit-directed life. It was really all about me! All I could think about was that I needed more love. When that didn't happen, over time, I blamed God. I thought I *deserved* better.

This went on for more than twenty years. Then at one point I decided to quit God. I just woke up one Sunday and said, "No, I'm not doing this anymore." I was so hurt and so disappointed that I just couldn't keep it up any longer. Then my husband and I decided to separate, and I decided to be a new woman. I had not dated many others in high school or college. So by golly I was going to do it now. And I did.

If only I had known then what I know now! For one thing, there is no such thing as greener grass. But that's not the half of it! If only I had known the truth about my Father God. That He loved me first. And so much so that He paid a huge price for my freedom. That He *always* wanted the best for me.

If only I had understood the reality of a fallen world. That I had carried bondages with me since the beginning, and I had not dealt with those issues yet. My revelation to that point in my life had been minimal, and I didn't even know these bondages existed! Even so, they had caused me to make poor choices and had limited my understanding of who God is and the kind of life He intended for me. They had kept me from loving and trusting Him first.

If only I had known how concerned God was about my problems and how much He wanted to help me break through to a higher level of living! Here's what I didn't get: my circumstances were not the issue. My lack of transformation was! But God couldn't push Himself on me or my husband or anyone else. I was not a willing party. I was not listening. His hands were tied.

Now I know that my Father God wanted to transform me. Wholeheartedness does not transform! What I needed was a new, soft heart—His heart—so I could become a channel through which His Holy Spirit power flowed to change things. That kind of understanding and power would have changed everything for me. A new heart and a new mind would have allowed me to finally rise above my circumstances and enjoy His presence and His greater purpose.

But I had no ears to hear. So I rebelled. Then I forgot about Him.

But praise God He did not forget about me! He pursued me. Relentlessly, He called forth the words that were lying dormant in my heart—the ones Satan had not been able to touch. "You are my daughter! I love you with an everlasting love! Let Me hold you in My heart!"

And so I heard Him calling. Finally, I decided to listen. He was patient and gentle. Forbearing. And very much a Shepherd! I was still a bit wayward. The One Thing still had a grip on me. I was still spending a great deal of time thinking about it and pursuing it, and making bad decisions in the process. But at the same time I was slowly developing a new attitude and a new mind and a new heart. I was saying new things. *I cannot do this by myself! Help me break out of this vicious cycle! I receive all the good things You are trying to give me!* When I would run off somewhere dangerous, He kept pulling me back in to Himself. There were many ups and downs, but He was always there with me.

> *The name of the LORD is a strong fortress;*
> *the godly run to him and are safe.*
> PROVERBS 18:10

Then came the most difficult period of heartbreak, when I lost the man I thought I would marry. But this time I did not let go of my Father God. I clung to Him even more. And I listened intently. He was giving me new revelations. In a dream one night He said He was transforming me into the image of Jesus. Then He showed me my destiny. It was far greater than what I had become! I felt like He was lifting me higher, and the Spirit's power was making me stronger.

That was when He showed me the shells. That's when I realized what He had been telling me the whole time. Finally, I was ready to receive it. He had always played second fiddle to the One Thing. He wanted to be the One to meet all my deepest needs. I had to run to Him first! With that revelation finally seen and heard, I began to let go.

Back in the Dallas Airport, I left Terminal A and headed out to Terminal C via escalator and the Sky Link—trying not to think too much about the guy whose mother was in the palm of God's hand! Down a long causeway I went. Then up the escalator to the Sky Link door. I stood for a bit—then happened to catch a glimpse of a lone bystander to my right. It was a dark figure, wearing earphones. Did I dare look up to make sure? Yet I already knew it was him.

There we were—just the two of us—waiting for the same train. No one else in sight. My heart smiled. God had done His part! He'd made it obvious.

I strode over to the young man, somehow overwhelmed with joy and excitement and near-panic all at once. I was fully expecting something amazing to happen. My approach caught his attention. Then he realized I intended to speak with him directly about something and removed the earphones.

I said, "Hello, this will probably seem like a really weird question, but are you on your way to see your mother?" He hesitated, then uttered, "No." There was a nervous pause. Then the silence broke. "I just came from seeing my mother," he revealed. With surety I responded, "I see. Well, this may seem bizarre to you—and I wanted to tell you this on the plane, I just felt awkward about it and couldn't tell you then. But here you are again! So I am going to tell you that God spoke to me when I was sitting there beside you. And He told me to tell you that He is holding your mother in the palm of His hand."

Transformed into the Life-Giving Image of God

In this world, there are receivers who operate in the truth. They are givers, not takers. They are God-focused and other-focused. And God consistently manifests His life-giving Spirit to others through them. Increasingly, they think and act like Jesus did. They love people and pray for healing. They don't see what is, but what can be. Everywhere they go, the kingdom increases and the darkness decreases.

These people are literally being transformed into the life-giving image of God Himself—the ultimate level of kingdom living that God intended from the beginning. How do they do it?

When we go straight to the presence of God with sincere hearts, fully trusting Him, Jesus's blood washes our consciences clean. Being clean and staying clean keeps the door to life open. Then the alive and active Word of God can penetrate our soft hearts. We receive revelation about the truth of God's Word when this happens.

Those who are transformed into God's life-giving image follow the recipe for a renewed mind and a changed heart—always careful to use the right ingredients and in the correct proportions! Consequently, they receive revelations that take them deeper and deeper into the heart and mind and presence of God. His words sink deep into their hearts where the enemy cannot go. This is how they *know* the truth about who they are and operate in that truth.

Satan has no hope of stealing God's words of revelation from these softhearted children who live in that secret place where God is. He can't even drive them to disappointment, frustration, or discouragement, because those things are no longer part of who they are. It's not about them anymore. They are free at all levels of being—spirit, soul and body—having released all the things that once held them back and kept them focused on themselves.

My journey has brought me to this point of revelation. Admittedly, it took a while to completely release the One Thing. But I did it, through the power of the Holy Spirit. And now God wants to use me to love, truly love other people just as Jesus did. I have His mind and His heart, which are being manifested in greater measures as I meditate on His words and go into His presence. And as I use my faith to go deeper, bypassing my selfish self, my fleshly desires decrease and His Spirit motivations increase.

I am being transformed! I am free indeed!

I will never forget that day in the Dallas Airport. When I shared what God had told me, the young man's stunned eyes widened, then darted down past my gaze. In slow motion, he nodded a few times. Then he half-smiled. He turned his face again toward mine, and our eyes locked.

"My mother just passed away," he told me. "I just came from her funeral. I am on the way back home to California now."

I can't recall if the Sky Link door opened and shut without our noticing or not. We stood facing one another, in a vacuum.

"Wow," I said. "Your mother is in heaven."

"I know that," he said. His dark eyes glistened. "I needed to hear that. I needed closure. Thank you so much for telling me that." The thank yous were repeated several more times. "By the way, my name is Sean."

He offered his hand. I told him my name. On the Sky Link I told him a bit about the book I had been reading, and how that was the first time I had ever received such a strong impression or word from God about a total stranger. He didn't say anything else, just nodded. He still had that baffled look.

Within moments, the train door opened again and we departed in opposite directions. Two strangers. But God knew us both. He allowed me to be the giver and Sean to be the receiver. I will not forget that encounter. I don't think Sean will either.

Discussion Questions

Look up the Scriptures listed and reflect on the questions presented. Possible "answers", along with Scripture references from the New Living Translation, can be located at the back of this book.

1. What is God's intention for us? (Hebrews 10:10; John 17:17–19; 2 Peter 1:3–4)

2. Transformation comes about through revelation, which ultimately changes us from within. What are the sources of this change process? (Ephesians 1:17–23; Ephesians 4:21–24; John 17:17)

3. How do we keep the Spirit's power active in our lives so our minds keep changing and we are constantly receiving revelation? (Hebrews 10:22; Hebrews 4:12)

4. How often can we go through the Gate (Jesus) and enter into God's presence? What do we find there? (John 10:9)

5. Revelation allows us to know the truth about ourselves, which sets us free from the power of sin and death. What is true about us? (John 1:12; Luke 3:38; Psalm 103:1–5)

6. What is the truth about our Father God? (Jeremiah 29:11–13; John 8:36; Numbers 6:24–26; Isaiah 64:4; Psalm 3:3; Isaiah 26:3; Psalm 139:5; Colossians 1:13; 1 Peter 5:6–7)

7. What is the truth about the counterfeit father? (John 8:44; Ephesians 2:1–2; 2 Corinthians 4:3–4; Revelation 12:9–10, 12; 1 Peter 5:8; 1 Corinthians 2:6–16)

Personal Reflections

1. Since you have been reading this book, what new things are you "seeing"? What if anything would you like for God to show you that you have not yet "seen"?

2. Is there anything in your past or present that you think might be still preventing you from hearing God speak? What can you now do to change this?

3. How would you describe the condition of your heart at this time in life? Chronicle on a timeline the various conditions of your heart since birth.

CHAPTER 6

REDIRECT

Now we can serve God . . .
in the new way of living in the Spirit.
ROMANS 7:6

Key #6: To live the kingdom life, we must consistently REDIRECT our focus and approach. It's this simple: run to Jesus. When we are with Him, automatic alignment with God's perfect will and purpose occurs. This is our created destiny.

MY MOM WAS PROPPED ON A PILLOW, slightly inclined, talking to me softly. I sat on the edge of the bed, leaning in, listening intently. I didn't want to miss a word. I had not seen her in four months, and now here we were in rapt conversation. I could not remember being so happy, so joyful, so excited to see her.

Mom's face radiated light. It struck me how calm and happy she was, though a tad groggy. But she was still coherent and so glad to spend time with me. I rubbed her leg with my hand. It was all good. She was telling me about her new living arrangement. Everyone in this place was wonderful, and the programs were very enjoyable. It was so peaceful, she told me. She was the happiest she had ever been. She could not have imagined a better situation.

Interjection. She needed to visit the restroom one more time. Would I go with her? Certainly.

Mom sat up, flung her legs over the side of the bed, and proceeded to stand. I was taken aback that she didn't have her left leg brace or quad cane by the bed, but she didn't seem to need either. I took her by the arm and we walked across the room with ease. I stayed close the whole time. I didn't want to let go. I was already feeling a bit uneasy that this bedtime ritual—though unexpected on this particular occasion—was drawing to a rapid close.

I tried to extend our visit as long as possible. But all too soon, she climbed back into the bed. She was so glad to see me, but it was time for sleep. So tired. I, on the other hand, was eager for more conversation. How long had we spoken? I wasn't sure. I'd been so engrossed in the sheer joy of her presence that I had somehow missed most of the details! Why didn't I prod her to repeat some of it? But she had already nestled down under the covers.

Like she did every time, she turned on one side and stuck out her arm. On cue, I had the perfume bottle ready and gave her a squirt. "I love you so much," she said. "And I'm so proud of you!"

My heart swelled. This was joy unspeakable. "I love you, too, Mom! I'll see you soon!" I bent down and kissed her on the forehead. She closed her eyes. The light dimmed.

Swoosh! The sound I heard suggested the sudden entrance of someone who had not been invited. I opened my eyes in my own bed and gasped. Hovering to the left of my bed was the outline of a demon's face and upper body, all blazing with fire—except for the eyes. He had hollow eyes. They glared at me. In my startled state, I felt only sheer terror and panic and helplessness. It seemed like it took me forever to respond. Like I was frozen. But in actuality, I quickly realized what I had to do. I elevated myself in the bed, raised my arm, and pointed a defiant finger. "In the name of Jesus, be gone!"

Immediately, the fiery figure vanished.

The Dreams that Stopped Hell

I lay there in bed, breathing heavily in the middle of the night, overcome with emotion. My mom—who had passed away four months prior—had just come to me in a dream. Joy incomprehensible! An instant later, I was terrorized by a demon who attempted to steal my joy. But he did not succeed. Instinctively, I had told him where to go.

I have had two dreams in the last two years that taught me something about how to redirect my life so I can more effectively love and serve God and others. Both times, the Spirit power in me literally stopped hell in its tracks.

This was the first of them. The other occurred several months ago after I started writing this book.

In the second dream, I was with Jesus. He was holding my hand, and He was pulling me into His heart. Our hearts were one. He was telling me about things that had been hidden—that He was going to entrust these things to me. My joy was the fullest it had ever been, because I was with Him, and I was completely yielded to Him in the Spirit.

In the dream, He told me He had been looking for a yielded heart. Someone with whom He could partner and so use as a change agent in the Big Story. He had singled me out many years ago, but recently, the time had come to give me deeper revelations and therefore more responsibility. He had a lot of work for me to do! Yet, He told me, the journey would not be arduous. It would be restful, because He would be doing the work through me. I did not need anyone else. He alone would give me all I needed for the journey. All I had to do was yield to the truth, adjusting and redirecting my focus and my approach to His along the way. In doing so, the work would stop hell in the lives of many people—one person at a time!

With that, I awakened. But the memory was fresh. I was overcome. Wow! I felt as if I had literally been in His presence. Perhaps I had! I thought for a moment about how amazing the experience had made me feel. I had been consumed with joy. He picked me! He was holding me close, in His heart! I could depend on Him alone!

Somehow, I had just touched the heavenly realm.

Then, suddenly, my mind reverted to reality. My journal reads, *Oh no! Does this mean I will never find the right man? That I will walk this path alone?* Surely He did not mean that! In my dream, a man had not mattered—not one iota. But now that I was living again in my flesh, the thought of spending the rest of my life without the One Thing— the right man—seemed rather disappointing.

The Focus that Stops Hell

When I was with Jesus in that dream, He had allowed me to see the unseen realm where He is. At the same time, my body, soul, and spirit were in complete alignment with His purposes for my life, my created destiny, because I was with Him there.

I believe Jesus took me to that hidden place in the dream because He wanted me to understand that, though it is uncommon for us to truly focus on the things of God, completely follow His lead, forget all distractions, and fulfill our destiny, it is possible. To the extent that I am willing to believe the dream and yield to the Holy Spirit, I can receive the grace I need to be there with Him here and now, in the secret place, regardless of my circumstances.

Being with Him gets me out of my own way. That's when transformation occurs and destiny is fulfilled.

My Jesus dream was yet another visual reminder: Stay with Him! He will keep you focused on the truth. You will not be deceived by the lies! His Spirit power will overcome your flesh—your mind and your will and your emotions! You will be transformed! Hell will be stopped! You just need to stay with Jesus in the secret place.

Let me turn this back on you, because the same things are all true for you: Where is the secret, hidden place with Jesus? Is it a literal place or a place where you go in the Spirit? Is it near or far? What is your focus there to be? What life triggers do you have that might warrant a trip to this secret place where God is? Do these questions give you any ideas as to how you might alter your approach in dealing with people or situations in your life that are difficult or stressful or disturbing?

Simply put, redirecting ourselves to the secret place is all about focusing on the new way versus the old way.

Let's refresh. Remember, as a race, our minds and hearts have been tainted since Adam. But God was at work in the Big Story, using people who would listen and act according to His plan. He was setting the stage for the new way of truth to appear. But first He had to set a standard, which He did through Moses and the laws for holy living.

When Moses went up the mountain to receive the law, God set in place for the first time the requirements to which His people needed to adhere—even though He knew they wouldn't be able to do it. Nonetheless, they needed to know what His justice and righteousness demanded. Later, they would understand the impossibility of meeting that obligation in their own strength. They would see the need to be in relationship with Jesus, the Savior, who would meet the requirement on their behalf. But they would also see their need for Spirit power. Only Spirit power could set them free from the guilt of not being able to follow the law on their own.

Feelings of guilt limit us. We cannot go any higher when we hit guilt. It is a ceiling. The Spirit removes guilt. Then we soar— because the freedom of the Spirit takes off the self-imposed limits and finally enables us to live a holy life!

So the truth about the old way of the law becomes clear: the old way exposes the fact that we fall short and shows us that we need to receive forgiveness through Jesus's blood shed for us. But the law by itself does not empower or motivate us to live the life God intends. Quite the contrary.

Even after we are born again, Satan understandably likes to keep our focus on the requirements of the law instead of on the Spirit's power.

First, he wants to relegate us to the "religious" camp, where we take pride in doing certain things or not doing other things—all of which keeps us from maintaining a close relationship with our Father God. In the religious camp, we are focused on doing rather than being. Our mindset is that we do things for Him instead of with Him. The problem with this focus is that it's all about us, not about what He has done for us and in us and is therefore doing through us!

So along we go. We are enthusiastic about our newfound faith for a while. But then it happens.

First, we might fall into some sort of sin that disappoints us and makes us feel like total failures. We are focused on meeting the requirements, remember? Or perhaps we have been plagued by some such sin from the get-go. We might manage to keep it under control for a period. And we might try to change and "do the right thing." But we keep failing, and we eventually come to obsess over our shortcomings. We feel condemned and powerless, so much so that sometimes we simply give up and go our own way—apart from the "religion" we once embraced. Of course, we might still feel a degree of guilt about the choice to do this. But we put up a good front.

Alternatively, we might stay tuned in to our religion but strive to cover up our problem. We live in guilt under the guise of religiosity. Again, we only fool ourselves.

With either outcome, the Christian life we are trying to live seems too hard, too extreme—not possible. And Satan is pleased about our rebellion or our inability to have an intimate relationship with the Father God. We are no threat to hell whatsoever! We are living in hell!

My friend, hell cannot be thwarted as long as we remain Spiritless and powerless. The answer is not in trying harder—that's what got us into this mess in the first place! The answer is in redirecting ourselves to the secret place. When you feel powerless to overcome a hurt, a problem, or a hang-up, go straight to the unseen place where

Jesus is. He loves you! He wants to show Himself strong in you. But He cannot work in you if your focus is on something seen.

So redirect. Run back into His presence, and your focus will realign with His. He will gently remind you concerning the truth. As a born-again receiver, your sin has already been removed! When the Father God looks at you, He sees Jesus. He sees righteousness. So no matter how many times you have failed, you can walk with a clean conscience. You can receive the Spirit power needed to move forward and discover the experience of fulfilling your created destiny.

Concentrate on knowing your Father God through relationship in the unseen place of His presence versus knowing Him through religious activities and meeting a laundry list of requirements. Then you will be ready and equipped for the next level of living: approach—becoming a change agent in the Big Story!

The Problem: We live in a fallen world. We have been deceived by a counterfeit father. We have bondages that keep us from breakthrough! We need revelation! Guilt is a lie and a ceiling that keeps us limited and trapped.

The Truth: My Father God loved me first. I am His daughter. He wants the best for me. He paid a high price for my freedom so I could become a believer and a receiver who has applied the blood of Jesus to her spirit, her mind, her will, and her emotions. I am set free! My guilt has been removed.

The Solution: I can go into God's presence and receive revelation concerning the truth. I can receive everything I need for transformation breakthrough. This is a place where I am always safe. Satan cannot go into the secret place! There, Jesus's blood washes me clean. Staying clean keeps the door to life open. Then the Word of God can penetrate my heart. I can become a

channel through which the power of the Holy Spirit flows.
I am a change agent!

The Approach that Stops Hell

When we learn the truth about ourselves, the channel to God's presence is opened wide and we begin experiencing His generosity toward us—His love, His mercy, His grace. That's when the Spirit power in us starts increasing and the negative power of the mind, will and emotions starts diminishing. And that's when we become givers, not takers—living for others instead of for ourselves. We are becoming full participants in the Big Story! Our focus has shifted!

Suddenly our circumstances become less burdensome. The grip we had on the One Thing isn't so tight. We may have even let go of it completely! Now the intimacy we have with our Father God is the most important thing to us. As a result, His presence in us automatically overflows to others, changing things up everywhere we go, bringing heaven back into human existence and stopping the advance of hell in the process.

"I tell you the truth, whatever you forbid [bind or lock] on earth
will be forbidden in heaven, and whatever you permit [loose or open]
on earth will be permitted in heaven."
MATTHEW 18:18

Through this redirection of our focus, we develop a new approach to life—the same one Jesus taught the disciples to use. It's an approach of unlocking the kingdom through use of authoritative commands. Remember, Jesus came to Earth in part to reclaim the authority that Adam had given away in the garden. Early in Jesus's life, He grew to understand the authority God had given Him. Later in His ministry, He set the pace, commanding powers and principalities in the unseen realm, and they obeyed him. As a result, He healed the sick, cast out demons, and ministered to the poor in spirit. Then He gave His disciples the authority to use these same keys to the kingdom—Spirit-induced commands that bind and loose heaven and hell, in effect unlocking the kingdom and bringing heaven back to Earth.

Later, all believers received this same authority. This happened when Jesus's blood was finally shed, the veil was torn, and all humans were given full and unlimited access to the power and authority of the Spirit. The resurrection set the record straight concerning whose authority on Earth was greatest!

Fifty days later, the early church was born. A dramatic unleashing of the Holy Spirit during a nationwide religious festival changed three thousand lives within a few hours' time. And what was the result? A dramatic decrease in demonic oppression and evil, as demonstrated through physical and psychological healings. Finally, a widespread receptivity of the Good News message, which then traveled to every end of the Earth.

> *On the day of Pentecost all the believers were meeting together in one place. Suddenly, there was a sound from heaven like the roaring of a mighty windstorm, and it filled the house where they were sitting. Then, what looked like flames or tongues of fire appeared and settled on each of them. And everyone present was filled with the Holy Spirit and began speaking in other languages, as the Holy Spirit gave them this ability. At that time there were devout Jews from every nation living in Jerusalem. When they heard the noise, everyone came running, and they were bewildered to hear their own languages being spoken by the believers. They were completely amazed. "How can this be?" they exclaimed "These people are all from Galilee, and yet we hear them speaking in our own native languages!" (Acts 2:1–8)*

And so, ignited by the Spirit's power, the early church leaders continued to utilize and teach all believers these authoritative commands taught by Jesus. Another amazing fact: the believers' authority at this time was even greater than when Jesus walked the Earth! The reason: the blood of Jesus had been shed, and the Spirit's power was operative and available to all believers in the fullest measure.

I have alluded to the fact that I did not grow up understanding the keys to the kingdom. Likely, neither did many of you reading this book. This is because Spirit power in the church was grossly eroded after its first four hundred years of existence. Unfortunately, the church had become more institutionalized by that time. "God access" had been limited. God had not changed! But the focus and the approach of the church apparently did. Christianity became more about buildings and organizational structures than it was about people and relationships and manifestations of God's power and love.

Remember, no Spirit and no application of Jesus's blood shed equals no power and no miraculous happenings. Physical healing and other manifestations of the Spirit, for example, died out almost completely in the early church and were not recorded again until the late 1800s.

But praise God, at that point the Spirit's power began to catch fire again! And since the turn of the twentieth century, manifestations have continued to grow in number. Since the 1960s, in particular, there has been further intensity, especially in Third World countries where receptivity is high. Now, people like you and me are responding in unprecedented numbers to God's call for change.

When the enemy appeared at my bedside and tried to steal my joy, almost instinctively I knew to take authority against him. I had been taught over the years that the name of Jesus is the most powerful weapon in our arsenal, and I had recently learned that commanding the enemy to be cast out in Jesus's name would get immediate results. I had become convinced that even if I couldn't literally see the enemy—perhaps I could only observe the effects of his presence in a person or a situation—I shouldn't be hesitant to command him to leave. But I had never—until that dream—seen a demon or felt the need to command one to go!

That experience taught me to recognize enemy practices when I saw them and then practice the approach Jesus taught. Now I tear down, cast off, release, or loose any stronghold or negativity that comes from the enemy's camp everywhere I go! I do this through the power of the Spirit and the power of Jesus's blood. I loose the bonds of pride, fear, lack of forgiveness, lust, deceit, selfishness, depression, anxiety, stress, condemnation, and physical illness or infirmities, to name a few examples. I do this both for myself and for others.

Let's get practical for a moment. This is how I dismantle the strongholds of evil: whether I am alone in my bedroom or praying in the presence of someone else, whether the words are spoken quietly or shouted out loud, I utter what is said as a command. I say, "I command (depression, anxiety, weakness or any other stronghold), known or unknown, to leave, to be dismantled in myself, my children and grandchildren, and/or any other person Jesus loves! NOW, in the name of Jesus! Because of the blood of Jesus. By the power of the Spirit. I have authority to command these things! Greater is He who is in me!"

Then comes the really powerful part. I speak the positive aspects of God into existence by binding the perfect will of God to myself and others I love. "In the name of Jesus, I bind my Father God's greatest purposes and will to myself, my children and grandchildren, and/or any other person Jesus loves! Our created destinies are fulfilled! The healing power of the blood of Jesus covers us all! Praise God! He manifests in us! Others see His glory in us! He changes the world through us!"

This is my declaration: I am a change agent. I have been given keys that unlock the kingdom of heaven and bring its power back to Earth! I can use the keys of the Holy Spirit's power and the shed blood of Jesus to loose or send away all darkness from my life and the lives of others. I can also use these keys to bind or tie up God's greatest purposes to myself and others within my sphere of influence.

Destroying Hell, Restoring Heaven

My dreams and other experiences over the last few years have confirmed in my mind and heart Jesus's key teachings about the Evil One and how I am to handle him. For starters, Satan is real. In my dream, he was seen. But he is mainly living and active in the unseen world. His purpose is to steal from us—even kill and destroy us—because we are made in God's image. He wreaks havoc in the lives of people all around me, many of whom I know well and love dearly. Countless others of his victims dwell within my sphere of influence, people I call on daily in my job, people for whom I pray at Christian Healing Ministries, and even people I might pass on the street or in the grocery store. Perhaps someone I am sitting beside on a plane!

God is love. He is greater than we can imagine. And He hates evil and wants to destroy its effects on Earth. That's why He sent Jesus. Even so, He is not a puppeteer. He has given us choice. And He will only move through people who have yielded to the truth about the Spirit's power and chosen to participate in the Big Story. As long as I am willing to be a change agent, He will equip me to fight the enemy in the unseen realm and then change the world—one person at a time, starting with myself.

I can keep my focus in line with His when I go straight to the secret place where Jesus is. There He lets me see those things which have been hidden. And He gives me everything I need. I am equipped to follow Jesus's approach and use the authority He has given me to counteract the negative powers I see in myself and others. I also speak the Word and power of God into my life and others. In doing so, I change. The people and situations around me change. I don't hesitate to use my authority. I love people and want them to walk in freedom, and they find freedom because the Spirit power that flows out of the heart of God goes to them through me!

Remember, Jesus came so we could once again manifest God's love and fulfill our created destiny as empowered change agents, helping others find and receive wholeness and healing of body, mind, and spirit! Jesus showed us how to find and keep the focus we need to get the job done. He gave us an easy approach that can be applied in about any situation. Now, together, we can effectively stop Satan in his tracks and help restore the kingdom of heaven on earth.

We are glad to do it. Our motivation is simple: when our created destiny is being fulfilled, we are peaceful and joyful. Our lives have purpose. Our circumstances do not define us or determine our happiness. Increased revelation and understanding keep changing us and inspiring others. We stay excited about the future, and we show others how they can live in the same way.

> . . . When the enemy shall come in like a flood,
> the Spirit of the LORD shall lift up a standard against him.
> ISAIAH 59:19 (KJV)

This Is Salvation

When we redirect our approach and let Spirit power flow from the secret place out to the world, we bring God's "salvation" to those around us. According to *Strong's Dictionary and Concordance,* the Greek word *sozo*—to save, i. e. deliver or protect (literally or figuratively); heal, preserve, save (self), do well, be (make) whole—is used interchangeably in the New Testament as it relates to salvation, physical healing, emotional healing, wholeness, and deliverance. In other words, Jesus didn't come only to make sure we get to heaven. He set about to make people whole—body, mind, and spirit. He "saves" us to the utmost—even in the twenty-first century!

Spiritual Salvation: "But everyone who calls on the name of the Lord will be saved [sozo]" (Acts 2:21). "And she will have a son, and you are to name him Jesus, for he will save [sozo] his people from their sins" (Matthew 1:21). "God sent his Son into the world not to judge the world, but to save [sozo] the world through him" (John 3:17).

All Dimensions: "He saved [sozo] us, not because of the things we had done, but because of his mercy. He washed away our sins, giving us a new birth and a new life through the Holy Spirit" (Titus 3:5). "Therefore, he is able, once and forever, to save [sozo] those who come to God through him. He lives forever to intercede with God on their behalf" (Hebrews 7:25).

Emotional Wellbeing: "Suddenly, a fierce storm struck the lake, with waves breaking into the boat. But Jesus was sleeping. The disciples went and woke him up, shouting, 'Lord, save [sozo] us! We're going to drown!'" (Matthew 8:24–25).

Physical Deliverance: So I want to remind you, though you already know these things, that Jesus first rescued [sozo] the nation of Israel from Egypt, but later he destroyed those who did not remain faithful" (Jude 1:5).

Mental Wellbeing: "Then those who had seen what happened told the others how the demon-possessed man had been healed [sozo]" (Luke 8:36).

Physical Healing: "For she thought, 'If I can touch his robe, I will be healed [sozo].' Jesus turned around, and when he saw her he said, 'Daughter, be encouraged! Your faith has made you well [sozo].' And the woman was healed [sozo] at that moment" (Matthew 9:21–22). "Such a prayer offered in faith will heal [sozo] the sick, and the Lord will make you well. And if you have committed any sins, you will be forgiven" (James 5:15).

Discussion Questions

Look up the Scriptures listed and reflect on the questions presented. Possible "answers", along with Scripture references from the New Living Translation, can be located at the back of this book.

1. Why did Jesus come to earth? (1 John 3:8; John 8:36; Romans 8:1–4, 15)

2. Before the crucifixion, how did Jesus go about redirecting people to their Father God? (Matthew 9:35–38; Luke 19:1–10; Matthew 9:1–7; Luke 18:35–42; Matthew 9:22; Luke 8:36) Who gave Him authority to do these things?

3. What did Jesus give His disciples the authority to do? (Matthew 10:1) Who did He later send out to do the same? What did Jesus tell the disciples concerning the work that God had given them to do? (Luke 10:1–9) What did Paul do? (Acts 28:8–9) What did Jesus say would be true of anyone who steadfastly believes? (John 14:12; Ephesians 1:19–22) What does James tell us to do? (James 5:13–16)

4. What happens when we pray with authority? (Matthew 18:18) Why must we exercise our authority? (Ephesians 6:12)

5. Our Father God wants to love lost and hurting people through us! But to be a conduit of God's love, we must qualify. What must we have? (John 10:10; 1 John 5:11-12; 1 John 4:11–13; Psalm 103:4; 1 Peter 3:22)

6. When we use our God-given authority, we become change agents. Then we can show others how to do the same. (Revelation 5:9–10; 1 Peter 2:9) How can we reign over sin and death? (Romans 5:17; John 3:27–30; 1 John 4:4)

Personal Reflections

1. Is there anything in your life that Jesus's power *to sozo* has not yet been applied?

2. Who within your sphere of influence needs to receive healing in one of the areas listed above? How might God desire to use you as a change agent in that person's life?

3. God needed the help of Moses and Abraham and others because He mainly works through people to accomplish His objectives. So He gave them authority. What has God given you authority to do?

CHAPTER 7

REJOICE

You honor me by anointing my head with oil.
My cup overflows.
Psalm 23:5

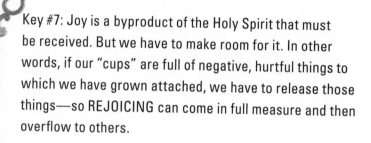 Key #7: Joy is a byproduct of the Holy Spirit that must be received. But we have to make room for it. In other words, if our "cups" are full of negative, hurtful things to which we have grown attached, we have to release those things—so REJOICING can come in full measure and then overflow to others.

THERE IS NO SUCH THING as a half-full cup. Our cups are always full. Of what? The things to which we are most attached.

A year and a half ago my cup was so full of the One Thing that there was little room for anything else. So when my relationship went awry and I was left with heartache, my cup overflowed with hopelessness and despair. I'm fairly certain there was not one ounce of real joy in me to dispense. Sure, the One Thing brought plenty of happiness while it lasted. But when the circumstances changed, I saw how quickly happiness can dissipate.

By contrast, I have learned that true joy is not dependent upon circumstances. I didn't always know this experientially, but I have

103

discovered it—through my trial. In fact, I have learned more about joy in the last year than I had learned in a near lifetime!

Ironically, it is the week before Christmas as I write these words. And though I formulated the outline for this book seven months ago, when Christmas was not even on the radar, I sit at my computer writing a chapter entitled "Rejoice" as "Joy to the World" rings in my ears.

> *Joy to the world! The Lord is come!*
> *Let earth receive her king!*
> *Let every heart prepare Him room!*
> *And heaven and nature sing!*

Wow! There are messages about joy in this carol I have never really heard before today. But these are the truths about which I intended to write!

My friend, joy, the oil that gladdens and comforts the soul in even the worst of circumstances, is a byproduct of the Spirit's power. This means it must be received. We can't create it by ourselves; it's a gift from God. But we also have to make room for it. In other words, joy does not magically appear without revelation received and willing sacrifices made. Demonstrations of faith and obedience must occur.

As an example, the biblical account of young Mary, the mother of Jesus, explains how true joy can be obtained. You may recall that the angel Gabriel appeared to Mary to explain that God chose and favored her to bear the Savior of the world. And at first, Mary was afraid, confused, and even disturbed. Who wouldn't be? This news was radical and totally unexplainable. An unmarried teenager would carry a child, but there would be no sexual relations involved? Would family, friends, and fiancé understand or even believe the story concerning this marvelous encounter?

Humble Mary immediately made room in her life for God's plan. However, it wasn't until days later—when she finally realized the magnitude of what God was going to do through her—that joy flooded her soul!

The Pathway to Joy

Though Mary's carrying of baby Jesus was culturally unacceptable, she was ultimately able to rejoice because she confidently aligned herself with God's highest purposes for her life. But to get there, she had to take initial steps of faith. She had to trust God's nature. Only then was He able to give her a deep revelation concerning what He was in the process of doing. Unspeakable joy was the byproduct.

The pathway to true joy should never surprise us if we let Mary's life be our example. We must remember that God's nature never changes and can always be trusted. He will get us to the end of the path when we trust Him. But at the same time, His ways and means can be unpredictable.

Four years ago I started down a pathway that I thought was leading to a place called "God's favor." I certainly didn't know that another long period of heartache and disappointment would be required to get there! But you already know what happened right before the time of the shells. And you already know that God ultimately used my heartbreak to push me to the level where I needed to be! Praise God He did! Otherwise, I might have never found the true joy that I'm writing about today.

At that time, I had been studying various Big Story participants who were considered "anointed" or "chosen" or "favored" ones. These individuals include Noah, Abraham, Moses, Mary the mother of Jesus, the apostles, and scores of other participants—way too many to list completely. Though most of them were humble, ordinary people with no special talents or abilities, God saw that these individuals received the assistance, the advantages, and the preferential treatment they needed to get various Big Story tasks completed. Needless to say, God was always doing big, outrageous things through these most favored participants!

And so, I decided that I wanted this same kind of exciting and favored life for myself. I had already begun to recognize the truth— that as a child of the Most High God I could declare or speak the truth about God's power in my life. Such declarations—calling things that are not as though they were—work to both renew our minds and stir the heart and hand of God.

So I composed a personal declaration, which I repeated to myself every day.

My Personal Declaration: *My life is significant! I use my gifts for the greater good of mankind and to give glory to God for all He has done—and for all He continues to do—as I live in His favor. I am blessed to be a blessing!*

My journey of declarations and affirmations had begun. But I must admit there was a bit of faulty thinking on my part. For instance, I wrongly assumed that God's favor was somehow tied to my possession of the One Thing!

Nonetheless, God was still there. And He was listening to me and working with me. I didn't realize to what extent, and I didn't realize just how much patience was required on His part. But I know now that He took me very seriously. He was slowly but surely making a way for my declarations to become reality.

Little did I know that He would ask me to relinquish my possession of the One Thing so as to make room in my cup for other things of His choosing. Nor did I understand that He intended to change things up a bit and possess me, instead of me possessing it!

But for sure, at the time of the breakup, I knew God had deliberately intervened and pulled me back to Himself. He had pushed the reset button and forced me back into alignment with His purposes and will. And so I had to choose. Would I trust Him or not? I believe He knew all along that I would. He knew I was ready to receive the revelation He was giving me—that I would have eyes to see the breakup as part of His favor. I couldn't exactly see where He was going with it, but it didn't matter. My heart was finally right!

That was the day my transformation process kicked into high gear. However, I was heartbroken. I thought I had absolutely no joy. And I knew I needed it. With no joy—no oil to soothe my wounds and revive my downcast spirit—I could not survive the test.

Thank God I knew to acknowledge Him as the Supplier of all good things! And to receive! By faith, I immediately started receiving joy. Out loud, over and over again I repeated, "Lord, I receive joy! I receive joy!"

Now please understand, I did not feel joy. Not one bit! But I kept receiving it. "I receive joy! I receive joy!" These Spirit-directed words touched my mind over and over again as I repeated the phrase. All day long I thought about joy. All week long. I even looked up all the verses in the Bible that referenced joy. I wrote out my favorites on notecards and carried them around in my car so I could repeat them over and over again.

Finally, after about two or three weeks, my declarations paid off. I was out on sales calls—I remember that particular day was a rough one—but I was still affirming joy and still forcing a smile. Boom! God placed a visual of joy right in front of my sad face—a woman named Flora.

Flora and her husband happened to be among my appointed sales calls for the day. I was visiting with them about final expense insurance at their kitchen table. She was an elderly woman who had a respiratory disorder and struggled with almost every breath—yet she was full of life and enthusiasm, clearly one of the most joyful people I have ever met. She was the kind of person whose physical limitations went almost unnoticed because she didn't draw attention to herself or to her infirmity whatsoever.

We had barely gotten into a bit of small talk when I commented about Flora's warm enthusiasm. It was contagious! Immediately, her husband asked if I could guess which Fruit of the Spirit Flora was known for.

I almost laughed out loud. Joy?

God does have such a sense of humor! And He is so good! There I was, desperate to receive joy, and He arranged to seat me in the presence of a lady whose life was the epitome of it—a soul who rarely ventured farther than the kitchen table but whose daily routine involved connecting with people all over the world through letters and phone calls and poems. Someone willing to use her dying breath to reach out, to encourage. Always giving. Always grateful.

I hung around for a while in Flora's kitchen and allowed her to minister to me. We shared our spiritual journeys. She read me a poem she had written as a tribute to an old friend. At her insistence, I picked up the phone and called a friend of mine who grew up in Flora's hometown in South Carolina. They chatted on the phone for a bit and recalled a few family names and area locations. Flora got the biggest kick out of that! When I finally got up to leave, she expressed her joy in meeting me. She invited me to come back for another visit.

Then she exclaimed, as though she were about to burst, "See that banana over there on the counter? I want you to have it!"

Joy is spontaneous!

The Increase of Joy

After I left Flora, I knew that God had sent me to this woman—not to sell insurance, but to receive something far greater: the truth about joy. And it was coming forth! I could feel joy welling up within me!

I knew I was on the right track and was starting to get excited about my newfound joy, but I sensed that patience would still be required. I must wait for God to work and develop in me the deep, deep capacity for joy that I had just witnessed in my new friend, Flora.

And then suddenly it happened. A totally new understanding about joy came over me. It was a thought I had never before conceptualized, related to a Bible verse about joy that I had quoted my whole life but never quite understood. Oh my! I opened myself up to the idea a little more. If I could learn to embrace my hardships—like Flora had learned to do—I would develop endurance. And in developing endurance, I would increase my capacity for things that I really needed in life, things like joy! It was very similar to training for a marathon.

Dear brothers and sisters, when troubles come your way,
consider it an opportunity for great joy. For you know when your
faith is tested, your endurance has a chance to grow.
So let it grow . . . for when your endurance is fully developed,
you will be perfect and complete, needing nothing.
JAMES 1:2

I was starting to get it! Just as marathon training develops lung capacity and muscle strength, hardship training—when we allow it to do its work—develops Spirit power capacity. And like a well-trained athlete's lungs and heart rate quickly recover from an intense run, a person trained by hardship can endure the ups and downs of life with relative ease. And she rejoices in the process!

This is how people like Flora manage to never become consumed or embittered by their circumstances. Over and over again, they permit trials to drive them to a place where they are utterly dependent on God to meet their deepest needs. And He always does. When they see that He does, this gives them joy. They are full, satisfied, complete—the way one feels after a good meal! They need nothing, just like the verse says!

The Surprise of Joy

I had seen true joy in Flora, and I knew I would find it too. So I kept pursuing. I felt just like the wise men, the Magi, who saw a new star. God gave them a revelation concerning the star's significance, and with no hesitation, they decided to travel thousands of miles to find Jesus. It took them over two years to get there, but they never quit.

And so as I was running along the beach one day, soon after I met Flora, I saw the shells. That's when I had my revelation. And then joy popped up and surprised me. I had been seeking it . . . but I was still surprised when it happened.

It was almost unbelievable to me! It was the revelation God gave me concerning my attachment to the One Thing that gave me joy—the revelation itself! God was asking me to release the One Thing so there would be more room in my cup for the fullness of His Spirit power. That was how God would meet all my needs.

I was so touched that God would take the time to respond to me in such a clear, manifest way. That He would let me know how much He loved me, how much He cared—how much He wanted me to experience the fullness of life that was available to those willing to put Him first, above all else. I was overwhelmed with joy! I was free!

At that moment, I knew I could trust His heart, His character, His nature. I was certain I could trust Him to be my Husband, my Strong Tower. I could run to Him and be safe!

Later, He gave me my assignment. *Tell other women who are hurting that they can run to me too. That I am the source of all good things. Favor and power. Joy, peace, and freedom. Tell them, and your joy will increase even more!*

I took in all these things, and I pondered them in my heart. I told my friends about the shells. I wrote the poem so I could remember. Then they read the poem. Many wept. Then God said to write this book. And so I began. He also said to become a prayer minister at Christian Healing Ministries, and so I did.

I can tell you without hesitation today: my joy is full!

Empty Your Cup

Dear reader, don't let your attachments separate you from true joy! Make room in your cup now! The Spirit's power will fill your cup to the point of overflowing with all the good things that come straight from the kingdom of heaven!

In this book, I have laid out keys or steps to living your life from the secret place and receiving purpose, freedom, and joy. You must follow the steps. Affirm and receive! Release! Embrace the training! It's a marathon we are running, not a sprint. I had to release the One Thing and embrace singleness. Your sacrifices will be different on the surface, yet essentially the same.

Here's the truth: whatever your sacrifice, it will seem minimal in comparison to what God will give you in return. You will see! He will give you everything you need. You will be whole and complete. Lacking nothing!

And joy will continue to develop and increase within you.

Then, you will discover the greatest Joy miracle of all. You probably won't be aware of it at first. But joy from your cup will start spilling out onto others. You will be surprised and delighted to see how God uses you to transfer joy, just like Flora did for me.

Lastly, once joy is received and cultivated and increased in your life, you will find that it is not carelessly lost or cast aside—or stolen. It is protected and guarded. For joy always proves to be that valuable—like a treasure hidden in a field. And you are willing to give up everything else just to own that field.

Discussion Questions

Look up the Scriptures listed and reflect on the questions presented. Possible "answers", along with Scripture references from the New Living Translation, can be located at the back of this book.

1. Jesus said the kingdom of God is like a treasure hidden in a field. (Matthew 13:44) A man found it and was overcome with joy. Do you think he was surprised to find it? What was the man then driven to do?

2. What is the kingdom of God? (Romans 14:17) Where is the kingdom of God? (Mark 1:15; Luke 17:20–21)

3. When we seek God, how does He surprise us? (Mark 4:22–24; 1 Corinthians 2:10–12) Do these kind of surprises increase our joy?

4. When Jesus was on Earth, He revealed the truth about God and showed people how to stay in line with God's greatest purposes. What was the byproduct of such revelation? (John 15:11; Proverbs 2:6–12)

5. What we think about and what we say out loud determines the condition of our hearts. The Word of God is truth. If—through meditation on the Word of truth (Joshua 1:8; Hebrews 4:12) and speaking the truth out loud (Proverbs 18:21; Matthew 12:37)— your mind changes through revelation, what will happen? (Luke 6:45; Deuteronomy 30:14)

6. After Jesus gave authority to the original twelve disciples, He sent them out to heal the sick and cast out demons. Later, He gave seventy-two additional people authority to go out on assignment. They too were to heal the sick and proclaim that the "kingdom of God is near." What did these folks report upon return? What was their state of mind and heart? What were the truths revealed which had been previously hidden? To whom are such truths revealed? What was Jesus's response to the revelations these people had received? What value did Jesus place on such revelation? (Luke 10:17–23)

7. When we are without joy, what are we to do? (John 16:24; John 15:5–8; Psalm 103:1–5; Philippians 4:19)

Personal Reflections

1. What (or perhaps who?) in your life might you quit fighting and begin embracing?

2. What steps might you take as a show of faith that God can and will give you everything you need for your journey?

CHAPTER 8

REPEAT

[Jesus] replied, "You are permitted to understand the secrets of the
Kingdom of Heaven, but others are not. To those who listen to my teaching,
more understanding will be given, and they will have an abundance
of knowledge. But for those who are not listening, even what little
understanding they have will be taken away from them."
MATTHEW 13:12

Key #8: At all costs we must guard our hearts. For from the heart, our life flows. Guarding the heart is analogous to listening to God's voice. When we listen, our understanding increases. When we let our guard down, we risk losing our ability to hear. REPEATING the steps delineated in this book keeps one fully aligned with God's greatest purposes!

ALL JAWS DROPPED at the ladies' Bible study when I told them the truth. Ironically, I had vowed earlier in the day to my friend Joanne, "I will just sit there and not utter one word!"

Joanne had started the study a few weeks prior, and she had been pestering me to attend. I was hesitant. I hadn't been to church one time in the last four years! However, she was persistent, and so I finally relented.

It did not go according to plan!

There I sat, trying very hard to put on a plain, unaffected, inconspicuous kind of face. There were about seven or eight of us altogether, seated in a full circle. I was the only newcomer. Truthfully, I thought the leader was a rather brash person, rattling on something about the Second Coming—a topic about which I was not one bit interested. But it was all acceptable enough. That is, until she had the audacity to pose this question: What were we doing for the Lord while we awaited His return?

She directed the question to the person at her right. But when she asked the next gal in line what she was doing for the Lord, I realized her intent—to go all the way around! And that's when panic set in. Oh my gosh, what in the world was I going to say?

There were three ladies ahead of me when I realized that I better cobble together a response. I could hear them all listing the typical stuff—praying, reading the Bible, going to church, taking care of kids, feeding the homeless, evangelizing the neighbors. Agh! I tried to look calm, but I doubt I succeeded. These were my options: I could act shy and pass. I could make up something. Or—I supposed—I could tell the truth!

"Well," I began. It was my turn. "If you had asked me this question ten years ago, I could have told you any number of things that I was doing for the Lord." Was I really going to say this? Yes, I was! I was going to brag!

"Like all of you, I was a faithful Christian. I never missed church. I taught outreach Bible studies in my neighborhood. I went to prayer groups and small groups for years. I studied the Bible intensely. I probably know more about the Bible than most of you!" After that comment, I detected a bit of surprise, a little edginess.

Then I took the plunge. "The truth is, I have been separated from my husband for three years. And I have been involved with another man for that length of time." That was when the jaws started dropping. "I haven't been to church for about four years, and I haven't prayed or read the Bible for about that long." Long pause. They were recovering. More than a few of them nervously readjusted in their chairs.

"But," I said, "there is a void in my life that I know I cannot fill. And that's why I am here." I could hear them all sighing, almost in unison. They seemed to melt, their faces softening.

Afterward, I was the focus of everyone's attention. They all hugged me. They told me how happy they were that I had come—and how much they appreciated my honesty. They asked me to please, please come back.

And so I did—every week, for about three years.

The Transformed Heart Is Soft

The Bible says to guard your heart. Your life flows from it. In other words, the condition of your heart determines the course of your life—a spiritual principle set in stone since the beginning of time. If your goal is to experience the transformed life, or the destiny God intended for you, you must ask yourself a critical question: *to receive a transformed life, in what condition must my heart be?*

> *Guard your heart above all else, for it determines the course of your life. Avoid all perverse talk; stay away from corrupt speech. Look straight ahead, and fix your eyes on what lies before you. Mark out a straight path for your feet; stay on the safe path. Don't get sidetracked; keep your feet from following evil.*
> PROVERBS 4:23–27

When I first believed and received the free gift of salvation at nineteen, my heart was in the right condition. It was soft! I wanted everything God had promised to give me. I had no idea, however, what exactly that meant. I just figured I'd better get busy!

Because several of my strongholds involved overachievement and competition, I quickly fell into a very typical form of enemy control. Doing good works. Performance. Information. More information.

Trying to do the "right" thing. Trying not to do the "wrong" thing. Putting up a good front.

I wasn't necessarily aware of it, but performance and knowledge of the Bible became goals in and of themselves. In my subconscious, "success" in these areas elevated me to a level higher than others. I wanted to be a leader, and I knew that leaders needed to know more and do more. It was a vicious cycle that kept me distracted and not really paying attention to the deepest concerns of God's heart.

Yet, all the while, God was sending me cues. He wanted to transform my heart and life! And I did know a few people who had experienced such transformation. I noticed they were peaceful, caring, humble, and full of wisdom, and God used them for good. They depended on Him for everything. But I could never quite put my finger on how they did it. Maybe I never asked. Maybe I never listened. Maybe there were too many distractions and Other Things in my cup. Maybe I just felt more comfortable doing it my way!

And so my heart kept hardening—so gradually that I never even noticed or suspected it was happening.

Then life got really difficult, and I became more and more frustrated and disappointed. That's when I decided that I simply could not live the Christian life. The standard was too high. And with no operative Spirit power to lift me to a place where the Evil One could not touch me, my unsuspecting heart started to shut down. Eventually, I decided to quit God. I never renounced him. I still believed in Him. I just decided to shut Him off for a while. And that's when what little Spirit power I had was taken from me.

I realize now how and why that happened. I know I never intended for it to happen, but it did.

I was still confident that I was going to heaven. I understood that the actual blood Jesus shed on the cross made that possible—that His blood sacrifice covered me, because I had received Him. Remember the story of the red lipstick?

But even with all of my Bible training, I did not understand the implications of living in a fallen world and how that reality played into my own personal life. I did not understand the gift of Spirit power and how it could operate in my life—how it could lift me up and lead me to transformation. Furthermore, I didn't realize that my performance mentality had always thwarted my ability to listen.

I had developed a hard heart. God was still talking to me. And He was still pursuing me. But I was unresponsive. I did not hear anything He was saying.

The Transformed Heart Listens

Soon after I started going to the Bible Study, God began speaking to me again—in His typical fashion, in ways in which I would be sure to hear him. For example, one day I left my leather Bible out on the living room sofa—the Bible I had used for nearly seventeen years. It had always been one of my most cherished possessions, because it was full of notes written in the margins, a spiritual diary of sorts. I knew my way around in this Bible because I had used it so much. If I wanted to find something, all I had to do was remember where it was located. Top, right side, near the back. Lately, as I dusted it off and enjoyed getting back into a regular reading pattern, it was like becoming reacquainted with an old friend.

As I walked past the living room that day, I happened to notice out of the corner of my eye a mound of white fluffy stuff on the floor near the sofa. I went closer and inspected it. No! No! No! To my horror, my Bible had been shredded to pieces! My daughter Claire had recently rescued a baby pit bull who chewed everything in sight. Anything of value had to be tucked away or she would get it. I'd overlooked that when I somehow left my Bible out.

I picked up what was left of it from the floor. Not one bit was salvageable. The pup had chewed through the whole thing. Sobbing, I threw it all in the trash. Then God said, "Do not rest on your laurels. Forget it all and start over. "

When Claire got home and saw how upset I was she said, "Mom, I think God is just telling you to start over!" Yes, I had gotten the message! Loud and clear!

And so began a time of softening. Rethinking. Discovering new truths. Listening. Receiving. Then not listening so much again. I was still wayward. Relearning. Revisiting. Receiving again. There were a number of cycles. This all lasted about five years.

Then came the shells, and I finally started to truly hear all that God was saying to me. My heart was finally soft again. I was able to understand the problem—the One Thing. My soft heart *wanted* to release it. The Holy Spirit's power helped me, and I was free! I was trusting God first. He would be the one to meet all my needs. I ran to Him. I was high above, with Him. I was safe in His strong tower. And I was not doing anything—just being with Him.

The Transformed Heart Receives

After I found the shells, I realized that my companions, Receive and Release, had led me to amazing treasures—a transformed heart and a transformed life.

And so, my friend, I want to share with you several things that helped me understand and grow in these disciplines. I call them the "kissing cousins," much like the two shells nestled together on the beach. They work best when they go together!

Let me take you back to the beginning of my transformation journey. During the time leading up to the dissolution of my marriage, the overachievement game was long over. And now, five years into singleness, I was looking for the life of rest, power, and freedom I had been reading about with my new eyes. That's when I decided: if there is a life like that to be had, I am going to find it. That's when I started learning about God's favor, which cannot be earned. It must be received. Favor is a free gift, the same as salvation.

Right away, I starting receiving God's favor. I began to realize that God's favor had many different names. Grace. Spirit power. Joy. Peace. Love. Freedom. God showed me that any spiritual gift is part of God's unmerited favor. And as my revelation about God's favor increased, so did my list of things I wanted to receive. They were all mine to be had, and I wanted them all! So I received them all.

In chapter 7, I briefly described how I used notecards and affirmations to help me receive joy when I needed it most. But I had established the notecard practice long before that. Somewhere along the way, I discovered these notecards to be a very practical help in receiving the truth I needed for transformation purposes!

On one side of each card was written a verse. On the other side, a personal application. The idea was to carry these around so as to have them available to repeat out loud as needed. You see, speaking truth and receiving truth regarding our personal situations— over and over again, out loud—allows the Holy Spirit to change our minds, which in effect changes ours hearts and our lives.

At the time of the shells I had amassed a huge stack of notecards. Many of the originals I had printed and passed around to friends and family. As a reader of this book, you will have access to a notecard template online which will allow you to print these and many others I have designed for you to use in your journey to transformation.

But for now, here is an example of one that will help you. The message testifies to God's unlimited resources, which are ours to be had. But we must receive them! In the blank, you can write what specific gift, blessing, or fruit of the Spirit you desire to receive.

Verse: Ephesians 3:16–19. *"I pray that from His glorious, unlimited resources He will empower you with inner strength through His Spirit. Then Christ will make His home in your hearts as you trust in Him. Your roots will grow down into God's love and keep you strong. And may you have*

*the power to understand, as all God's people should, how
wide, how long, how high, and how deep His love is. May
you experience the love of Christ, though it is too great to
understand fully. Then you will be made complete with all
the fullness of life and power that comes from God."*

Application: *God loves me like crazy! And because He
loves me so much, He has created a way that I can tap His
unlimited resources—which allow me to live abundantly
with all the fullness of life and power! This is NOT a secret.
God's Word is clear. His strength, power, peace, joy, and
love (along with all good things) are constantly available
to me, His child. This truth can be confirmed daily through
my life experience. My job is to receive everything I need!
Lord, thank you! I receive _____!
You are giving me everything I need!*

The Transformed Heart Releases

Understanding and applying RELEASE magnifies what his "cuz"
RECEIVE has already started! Believe it or not, I first heard about
"releasing" when I was a college senior. But I never thought of using
it until after I joined the Bible study where the jaws dropped! An
acquaintance of mine named Mimi, who had taken a spring semester
abroad, returned to school the next fall with a remarkable change in
her demeanor. I couldn't comprehend it. She had been radically transformed. She went away with a hard, competitive, self-centered kind
of attitude and returned six months later soft and full of the Spirit.

When I inquired about her change, she explained that she had
been involved in a Christian fellowship in England where she had
learned to release all of her anxiety concerning some family issues
back home. Her parents were apparently divorcing. And since this was

before the days of cell phone coverage, she felt powerless to help the family through this ordeal. She had to relinquish control and entrust them to God's care. She cupped her hands together and explained to me how she would visually place her family in her hands. Then she would raise them up to God and visualize Him taking them from her.

This made such an impression on me at the time, I can't believe that I did not apply this spiritual discipline to my own life. Instead, I totally forgot it! Was my forgetfulness due to hardheartedness? Regardless, the release Mimi described eventually popped back into my head. And praise God it did! I started releasing things in my private time, yet I had no idea what effect this practice would ultimately have on me. It would change my life. Even so, I knew it was a valuable tool. So one night at the Bible study I told everyone about the power of releasing.

After I explained, my Bible study friends expressed their enthusiasm about the idea. Joanne suggested that I lead the group in a prayer. We all cupped our hands together. Then, step by step, I led everyone to the point where we would all silently release whatever issues or burdens weighed on our individual hearts.

Well, this release exercise was anything but silent! Before I knew it, several ladies started sobbing. By the time we released, one gal was wailing!

Little did I know then how very powerful release can be in terms of freeing up space—space that has been taken over by the things that have most consumed us. As you know, I would later discover the truth about release in a more personal way. But I'm happy that some of the ladies in the group that night experienced it to the extent that it really made a difference. Their tears provided evidence that they had finally made room in their hearts so the joy and freedom of the Spirit's power could enter and begin their transformation!

The Transformed Life Gives

When we release all negativity—all burdens, issues, strongholds, and addictions, along with anything else that pulls us down, steals our joy, or sends our lives to nowhere—we are able to receive the Spirit's power in full measure.

This force is so powerful we cannot contain it all. The Spirit's power that comes into us spills out onto others. God's Spirit spilled onto me through Flora. God's Spirit spilled onto the airplane guy through me.

Dear friend, run into the secret place of God's presence. Then release and receive your way to a transformed heart. When you do, you will automatically get a transformed life! Not only that, you will become a giver, because God is a giver. And you will wake up thinking about others, because that is what the transformed life does!

This is why God is favoring us and transforming us—because of others! It's not about us. Sure, we reap the benefits of peace and joy and love and power and revelation. But we don't have to prove anything by it. Our challenge is simply to responsibly use our God-given gifts to sow the life-giving Spirit into the lives of others. That's it.

There is only one hitch: We can't quit! We must REPEAT! As long as we sow the Spirit back into others, we build momentum and reap countless times. Our anointing of love, power, and revelation increases all the more as we use it. That's the spiritual principle by which we live, and God doesn't lie. His character never changes.

Soon after the shells, I became very aware of the needs of other women around me. They seemed to need and want exactly the same things I had just been given. They seemed to want the understanding I had received. And so I effortlessly began sharing what God did for me. Women in need popped up everywhere I turned!

When I wrote the poem and began sharing it, I had many a conversation with women about receiving and releasing, and about how I had learned to trust God to meet all my needs. The outcome of these teaching moments, I decided, was entirely up to God. It's never up to me to persuade anyone to do anything or believe anything that I am telling them. I just share my story and leave the rest to Him. His Spirit power will do the work.

The same thing goes for physical healing. I've started praying for people to be physically healed when I go out on sales appointments. Since I meet primarily with retirees, many of the folks I see are not in the best health. Many are lonely. Again, the outcome of my ministering is not up to me. I just use the measure of faith I have been given and leave the rest to Him. But the people who receive my prayers are certainly grateful. Their spirits are lifted to know that a total stranger could care about their situation! And of course, I leave them with the message that God cares. He loves them and He wants to meet their deepest needs.

The Point of It All

Jesus's shed blood wiped away the burden of our sin and provided us an opportunity to receive eternal salvation. But His blood also provided a way for us to become transformed and live a life of peace, joy, freedom, power, and love here on Earth! Jesus came to defeat the work of the devil and to show us how to do the same!

The science of human blood gives us fascinating insight into the work of Jesus's blood. Red blood cells give life to all parts of the body by providing oxygen and cellular food. They also carry off waste products to the kidneys, skin, intestines, and lungs. So a red blood cell distributes life-giving oxygen and nutrition and yet carries off garbage at the very same time. White blood cells gather together when there is an infection and go into fighting mode. Antigens in the blood prevent disease. Jesus's blood gives us access to God's Spirit power, which gives us everything we need to access the fullness of life! Sin-induced issues are removed as needed, and we maintain a clean spiritual system. In the process, we are released from the power of sin, death, and darkness. We are free to live a new life!

When we believe and receive all this Good News, the transformed life is possible! But we have to be willing to participate. If we choose to do nothing or to quit at some point along the way, we lose.

We must ask these questions: What must we do? And what must we receive so Satan is defeated and we are free to then live the transformed life? I believe the answer is threefold:

1. Run into God's presence and RECEIVE His heart. When a person believes and receives salvation, a new, soft heart comes with the package—along with Spirit power, status as a child of God, and all the other rights and privileges therein. All of these gifts are made available because Jesus's blood was shed on the cross. Realize: everything has changed for you because of Jesus's perfect shed blood, which destroyed the separation between mankind and the Father God and released the fullness of Spirit power. As a believer and a receiver, you have direct access to this transforming power!

2. RECEIVE God's words. Then speak His truth into your life. The Bible says that our testimonies—our words spoken—change us, starting with our minds. Then our hearts change, and then our lives. When Truth is spoken, Spirit power is automatically released and applied. When we know the truth—and are in the habit of repeating it over and over—we see results. The bonus: Our spoken words change others too.

> *For with God nothing (is or ever) shall be impossible. (And no word*
> *from God shall be without power or impossible of fulfillment.)*
> LUKE 1:37, AMP

3. RECEIVE God's life. Die to yourself: in other words, release all the things that keep you focused on yourself. Do this, and His life and power will consume you instead. You will be transformed! When you are not afraid to completely let go of your One Thing and let God take over, the actual fabric of your life starts changing, and things start to get very exciting! The pull of negative thoughts

and emotions diminishes, and the Spirit's power becomes more and more dominant. Other people notice. You begin to fulfill your destiny. You begin conforming to Jesus's image.

Your life is no longer your own. God is living His life in you! You are a giver, because God is a giver. The Holy Spirit is flooding through you. It's not about you anymore! It's about others. Your heart is God's, and it focuses on others first. Everywhere you go, you sow Spirit power into others.

When you have used the eight keys presented in this book, you live in the secret place where God is. You live in His presence. Satan cannot touch you there. Your mind and your heart are protected. You are able to see things which were previously hidden. And your joy is full.

Maybe you have not believed this message until now, my dear reader and friend! Your life has been determined by the One Thing that has consumed you. The condition of your heart has stymied growth and expansion and revelation. Negative mental and emotional bondages and other distractions have dominated and determined your course.

But now your heart is soft and ready to receive all the good things God has been trying to give you. So just open yourself up and do it! If you have read and studied to this point, you know there is nothing whatsoever you can do to earn any of it! So just receive! Then let the Spirit power do the rest. You won't know exactly what the result will be. But that's part of the fun! His ways are totally unpredictable. He will surprise and delight you!

Here is the real point: God never changes! He is your security! You can trust Him! Believe Him and receive Him. Go to Him where He is. Taste and see that He is good. He will lift you high and protect you and defend you and transform you. He will give you everything you need!

Discussion Questions

Look up the Scriptures listed and reflect on the questions presented. Possible "answers", along with Scripture references from the New Living Translation, can be located at the back of this book.

1. Two voices constantly call to us. The Accuser's voice speaks death to us, while the Spirit, our Advocate, speaks life. What is the aim of the Accuser's remarks versus those of the Spirit? (Proverbs 14:12; John 10:10; John 15:26; John 8:1–11; 2 Timothy 1:7; 1 Corinthians 14:33; 2 Corinthians 10:3–5; John 10:27–30)

2. How do we block the voice of the Accuser and defeat any power that he is trying to have over us? (Revelation 12:11; Isaiah 59:19)

3. Why do we need to receive a new heart? (Ezekiel 36:26; Jeremiah 17:9)

4. God's Word is a book about life as it relates to Jesus's ultimate blood sacrifice. What understanding must we receive as it relates to the connection between these two things? (Leviticus 17:11)

5. How do we receive and manifest the transforming life of God? (John 12:24; John 14:16, 26; Hebrews 10:19–22; Ephesians 2:6–7; Hebrews 4:16; Matthew 10:8; Matthew 13:8, 23) What happens as a result? (Luke 6:38)

6. What did Jesus transfer to the woman who was caught in adultery? (John 8:1–11) Do you think she was transformed after her encounter? Did she leave the scene "clean" or "unclean"?

7. A blind man's friends took him to Jesus to be healed. (Mark 8:22–30) Jesus took the man to a place where there were no distractions. Then he spit on the man's eyes. What did Jesus then ask him? What happened after that?

Personal Reflections

1. Think again about the story of the blind man in Mark 8:22–30. What do you see, dear reader? Do you still see trees, like the blind man saw? Are you ready for the Spirit to take you to Jesus so you can receive everything He has in mind for you?

2. What do you perceive your created destiny to be at this point in your journey to transformation?

REST

Be still in the presence of the LORD and wait patiently for him to act.
PSALM 37:7

ONE AND A HALF YEARS AFTER I found the shells, at a point when I had nearly completed the writing of this book, a miraculous and wonderful event occurred that changed the course of my life—again. I had finally learned to run into the secret place of God's presence, a place I knew I could go and be deeply loved. It was a place of rest, where there was no striving, no need to prove anything, the place where all my deepest needs were sure to be met. I had learned the secret of truly enjoying His presence! And I was anxious for nothing. I was, however, *expectant* that something big was going to soon happen. God was going to act in some way, shape, or form. And it was going to be really good! I was sure of it. Yet I never imagined what God had in store!

At just the right time, God surprised me. Suddenly, almost without notice, the person I had previously lost—the same guy who broke my heart and drove me into God's presence—reappeared. While we were apart, he'd had a similar transformational experience. He was now ready to "embrace the training"— marriage training!

I had learned to trust God first. Then He gave me my heart's desire—an earthly husband who supports and embraces my journey into the healing power of God's presence. We are getting married next week!

The most life-giving relationships we can experience as humans are all about rest and healing—enjoying the presence of the other person, feeling assured that he or she has your best interests at heart. These relationships mimic the restful, peaceful, trusting, and loving intimacy we have with our Father God.

"Mimic" is a key word here. Please understand, Larry is an amazing, generous, and loving man. He inspires me. But he is not God. He will not meet my deepest needs all the time. Only God can do that. This is the lesson I had to learn before God could give me my heart's desire. Learning to rest in the secret place of His presence taught me this.

I wrote my vows to Larry this week. They reflect what I am talking about. I will vow my love and faithfulness to him, to tell him the truth always, bless and affirm him, and do my part to secure God's greatest blessings for him and his children and future grandchildren. But I will also vow this: I will never hold him responsible for meeting all my needs, all the time. I do trust him to try! I am confident he will do the very best he can with what he's got.

This is the truth and I know it: my Father God is the only person who is always reliable, always understanding, always giving, always loving, always kind. He is the One who always has my best interests in mind. He loves me more than anyone else, including Larry!

I am convinced that resting in God's presence is the only way we can find the best solutions to our life's problems. I am also convinced that learning to live and rest there in the secret place with Him will produce in us the greatest, most miraculous, most powerful, and most transforming results.

So come with me now, my dear friend! Let us invite the Holy Spirit to take us to this "not-so-secret" place where there are no limits! We will run and see Him there together! We can taste and see His goodness. We will lack no good thing!

*He who dwells in the shelter of the Most High will
remain secure and rest in the shadow of the Almighty
[whose power no enemy can withstand].*
PSALM 91:1, AMP

*Taste and see that the LORD is good. Oh, the joys of those who take
refuge in him! Fear the LORD, you his godly people, for those who
fear him will have all they need. Even strong young lions sometimes
go hungry, but those who trust in the LORD will lack no good thing.*
PSALM 34:8–10

*The high and lofty one who lives in eternity, the Holy One, says this:
"I live in the high and holy place with those whose spirits are contrite
and humble. I restore the crushed spirit of the humble and revive the
courage of those with repentant hearts."*
ISAIAH 57:15

*Two people are better off than one, for they can help each other
succeed. If one person falls, the other can reach out and help. But
someone who falls alone is in real trouble. Likewise, two people lying
close together can keep each other warm. But how can one be warm
alone? A person standing alone can be attacked and defeated, but
two can stand back-to-back and conquer. Three are even better,
for a triple-braided cord is not easily broken.*
ECCLESIASTES 4:9–12

Personal Reflections

1. What do you think about your relationship with God now? What
   have you learned in this book that will help you "rise up" to the lofty
   places where He is?
2. Can a good friend who knows about the secret place of God's presence help you go there?

A Prayer for You

I am satisfied to be/rest with You here in the secret place
of Your Presence. I am satisfied to allow You to love me.
I feel Your love. I feel Your embrace. I am satisfied to let You
pull me close into Your heart. My heart is one with Your heart.
My mind is one with Your mind. Our spirits are intertwined,
joined. I am content to trust You, to love You—to let You protect
me from people, situations, circumstances. I am safe here with
You. You are meeting all my needs—physical, mental, emotional.
Thank You, Lord, Holy Spirit! You don't judge me here.
You just love me! You lift me up!
I need peace. You are giving me peace, wisdom and
knowledge. I am addicted to You, Holy Spirit. Here is where
I can come to get disconnected from all darkness that has gripped
me. It is where all my unhealthy addictions are dismantled,
disconnected, leveled. And it is where You remind me that what
we have here, together, is what makes my life RIGHT.
Yes, it is because of You, Jesus, that I am RIGHT (or righteous).
What I know and experience here with You is always true
and RIGHT. It is my true identity. Thank You, Holy Spirit,
for reminding me. Bring me here often! So I can once again
REST and REALIGN myself with You and let You love me. So I
can learn to live in the destiny You have created for me.

An Affirmation

I am imagining for a moment that my life is a cup.
And it is full of many things. Some dark things, such as fear,
anxiety, selfishness, pride, addiction, offense (I have been
wounded or offended by someone), deception, sickness.
And I am sitting at your feet, Jesus. It's the secret place!
Yes, I am there with You! And You are eager to give me

*everything I need—EVERYTHING. But there is no room
in my cup. It is so full of these other things.
And so You are asking me to POUR OUT those
things that are dark (i.e. RELEASE) so as to make
room for all the things of Your choosing.
So I release the darkness. I give those things to You. I am
handing them over! You are dealing with these things for me!
I am making room in my cup. You are giving me peace,
confidence, joy, revelation, understanding, contentment, humility,
health, wholeness. You are giving me everything I need. And I feel
Your love, Your acceptance, Your kindness. My cup is now full of
those things. And my cup is overflowing those things to others.*

8 KEYS TO EXPERIENCING GOD'S PRESENCE

REALIZE: If we are stuck and consumed by problems, the life we live is not the one God intended—but a much higher level of living can be discovered and experienced. To begin discovering that life, we must REALIZE the greatest truths about God and His arch-enemy, Satan, the deceiver of our souls.

REROUTE: We are born into enemy territory, displaced, and disconnected from God's love. So we must REROUTE—turn from our own way of living life and follow His lead. When we make a conscious decision to do this, we become connected to His Spirit power and can begin hearing His voice.

RECEIVE: God's plan has always involved partnering with ordinary people to accomplish His work so we humans could be bought back from the power of Satan and restored to our original state as sons and daughters. When we believe and RECEIVE the Good News about Jesus, our identity as God's children is reinstated, with all the rights and privileges thereof. We then have access to the power and love of God. Satan's power over us can be thwarted.

RELEASE: God has made available to His children all the power needed to live the life of abundance He has promised. However, we must overcome nearsightedness, stubbornness, and hardheartedness through the RELEASE of bondages that keep us enslaved and unable to embrace our new way of life.

RENEW: Power flow occurs when we receive the same deep revelations that Jesus received, from the same sources Jesus tapped: the Word of God and the presence of God. We must follow the same recipe Jesus followed, starting with faith, then applying the Word and the presence in equal measures. The result is a RENEWED mind and a changed heart—a transformed life filled with peace, freedom and power.

REDIRECT: To live the kingdom life, we must consistently REDIRECT our focus and approach. It's this simple: run to Jesus. When we are with Him, automatic alignment with God's perfect will and purpose occurs. This is our created destiny.

REJOICE: Joy is a byproduct of the Holy Spirit that must be received. But we have to make room for it. In other words, if our "cups" are full of negative, hurtful things to which we have grown attached, we have to release those things—so REJOICING can come in full measure and then overflow to others.

REPEAT: At all costs we must guard our hearts. For from the heart, our life flows. Guarding the heart is analogous to listening to God's voice. When we listen, our understanding increases. When we let our guard down, we risk losing our ability to hear. REPEAT-ING the steps delineated in this book keeps one fully aligned with God's greatest purposes!

ANSWERS

Chapter 1

1. God has intended only good for us. He made us, He knows us, He pursues us, He blesses us, and He wants a relationship with us.

2. It offered eternity, blessing, healing, light (revelation), and authority.

3. The Knowledge of Good and Evil would cause them to "surely die." This meant they would become mortal and die a physical death. But it also meant they would die spiritually. In other words, their heart motivation would also be destroyed.

4. God made man in His image and breathed His own life into him. He also gave him authority over the earth, along with freedom of choice. Obviously, God did not "need" us. But He wanted us. He wanted to have a family! He is a relational God!

5. He loves us. We are precious to Him, and He wants to be with us. He helps us and protects us and saves us from destruction and oppression.

Chapter 2

1. God is love. His nature is to love us and to be faithful to us. He does not change. He is slow to anger. But He will discipline those He loves.

2. We are born sinful and separated from God. We tend to be wayward like lost sheep. We want to go our own way.

3. If we are sorry for our sin and turn and follow Him, our relationship with Him can be restored.

4. God's kindness is meant to lead to repentance. But because He is also just, severity will follow if there is no change in our hearts. He must punish sin.

5. He is consistent and reliable. He doesn't change. He is persistent, loving, and kind. But because there is no name higher than His, He can judge according to His standard as He wills.

Chapter 3

1. Jesus's blood was sinless because its source was God Himself. His "life" was sinless because His blood was perfect, untouched by the curse of sin that came about as a result of Adam's disobedience.

2. Jesus's sinless blood bought man back (or freed him) from Satan's slave market. His blood also removed sin once and for all. His forgiveness is so extensive that He remembers our sins no more.

3. We must believe that God raised Jesus from the dead and then confess with our mouth that Jesus is Lord.

4. Faith is an inner knowing that gives us assurance about things we cannot see. It comes to us when we hear the Good News!

5. When we have faith we experience new birth—and receive a new heart, a new life, and a new Father! We are also equipped to do things that would be otherwise impossible.

Chapter 4

1. A very thick curtain in the temple—one intended to keep people separated from God's presence—tore in two from top to bottom. Other signs could not have gone unnoticed: darkness, an earthquake, and dead people rising from their tombs.

2. Once and for all, Jesus's sinless blood secured our release from the penalty of our sin—and also the power of our sin! Now we can be forever clean. We are worthy to boldly enter into His presence at any time.

3. Jesus breathed on the disciples and told them to "receive the Holy Spirit." Perhaps this encounter was a foretaste of what would come later. In Luke's account, He tells the disciples to wait at the same location, because at a later time the Holy Spirit would come and fill them with "dunamis" power.

4. He is seated beside the throne of God in heaven. He intercedes for us. He disperses Spirit power to us. He ministers to us when we come to Him.

5. We should expect to live a life that demonstrates God's operative "dunamis" power. This power overrides our inherent weaknesses. It enables us to do things in life that we would never be able to do in our own strength.

6. First, we embrace (accept) God's command to love one another by way of our true Father and His Son, Jesus. Then we receive the Spirit's power. We trust our Father God. And our roots grow deep into His love.

7. It comes from God's Spirit. He is the one giving us the desire and the power to do what pleases Him!

8. Which came first, the chicken or the egg? In other words, don't try to figure this out! Just dive in and receive all that God wants to give you! Release of the Spirit's power will then come in full force.

Chapter 5

1. God intends for us to be transformed—and thereby empowered to do His work and participate effectively in His Big Story.

2. The Spirit and the Word of God are the sources of holy transformation. In combination, they change our minds about who we are so we can receive our new nature.

3. To keep Spirit power active, we go straight to the presence of God, with sincere hearts, fully trusting Him. There, Jesus's blood washes our consciences clean so we receive revelation about the truth of God's Word.

4. We can enter into God's presence as often as necessary to find safe pastures where the enemy cannot harm us. Preferably, we learn to live there! This is where we can hear God's voice!

5. God is our Father—just as in the very beginning! As His children, we inherit all of His divine benefits. These include forgiveness of sin, physical healing, release from the power of sin, ability to become change agents, and satisfaction and fulfillment in all things (i.e. transformation).

6. God reveals Himself to us. He has a good plan for us. He made a way for us to live in freedom. He blesses and protects us and favors

us. He answers us. He goes before us and after us. He holds our heads high. He delights in doing things for us. He keeps us in perfect peace. He cares about us. He rescues us and transfers us to a new kingdom.

7. Satan is a murderer and a liar. He is the ruler of a kingdom that is opposed to our Father God. He is at work in those of us who are disobedient. He condemns us and judges us and accuses us. He is filled with fury. He steals and kills and destroys. He deceives. He tries to keep the truth about our Father God hidden from us.

Chapter 6

1. Jesus came to destroy the works of the devil so we could become God's children and be set free from the power of fear, sin, and death. Ultimately, He achieved this end through His death and resurrection.

2. He restored them to wholeness by loving them, showing them compassion, forgiving them, "saving" them, healing them, and casting out demons everywhere He went. God gave Him the authority to do these things.

3. Jesus gave His disciples authority to cast out demons and heal every kind of disease and illness. Later, He sent out seventy-two more believers to minister and heal the sick. Believers now do even greater works since Jesus has gone to the Father, because the Holy Spirit has been unleashed in full force. All believers can pray and anoint the sick with oil, and they will be healed. All believers are equipped to do the work He is calling them to do.

4. We bind or lock up (to "bind as in bond, knit, tie, wind") those things which cannot be seen. Also, we loose those unseen things ("break up, destroy, dissolve, melt, put off"). We are not fighting

against flesh-and-blood enemies, but against the powers of evil in the unseen realm.

5. To love people like Jesus did, we must be filled with God's life, which comes from His Spirit. *Zoe*—the Greek word used in the Bible for "life"—literally means "the life of God." When we are filled by God's life, love, and Spirit, we can walk with the authority that still belongs to Jesus in the heavenly realm. But we must grow up into this understanding: that God has already crowned us—i.e. given us authority—the same as He would a king. When we understand our God-given authority, we can become active in using it! True authority is administered with tender mercy and loving kindness.

6. Through God's grace—His unmerited favor—we can reign as kings and priests over sin and death. As kings, we have authority to change things in the spirit realm. And as priests we are equipped to serve others and show them how they too can walk in authority. When this free gift of grace is continuously received and applied, the life and love of God increases in us, and the desires of our negative mind, will, and emotions decrease. Likewise, our authority increases. We become stronger than the world around us.

Chapter 7

1. The discovery of joy was likely unexpected. But because the joy this man found was so rare and valuable, he quickly changed all his plans. He sold all he possessed so he could buy the field and keep the treasure. True joy affects people that way!

2. The kingdom of God is goodness and peace and joy in the Holy Spirit. It is near and accessible to those who reroute, believe, and receive the Good News!

3. He reveals those things which have previously been hidden from us.

4. Joy!

5. Through revelation, your heart will change. You will be transformed from the inside out. What comes out of you will be different. What is in your heart is on your lips!

6. "Even the demons obeyed when we used your name!" The disciples were full of joy! The disciples grasped the truth: we have been given authority over the enemy. He cannot hurt us. We know the Father's heart and mind through Jesus. Jesus placed the highest value upon these revelations regarding our power over the enemy. Even the prophets who wrote about the future did not fully understand these truths, which could not be revealed until they were fulfilled in Jesus.

7. Ask and receive, in Jesus' name! Speak the truth about God's purposes and receive your inheritance! Run into His presence and He will give you everything you need!

Chapter 8

1. The Accuser's words are meant to incite condemnation, confusion, fear, intimidation, argumentative behavior, pride, rebellion, bondage, and death. The voice of Jesus, who is our Good Shepherd, along with the voices of the Spirit and the Father God, are merciful. Their voices bring forth confidence, abundance, blessing, understanding, love, peace, self-control, life, and transformation!

2. We defeat the enemy by raising the *standard* of Jesus's sinless blood and applying it to every situation, by speaking the truth of God's Word, and by confirming the truth through our testimonies. We also defeat

the enemy by overcoming the fear of dying to ourselves and becoming givers of God's life in us to others.

3. Our old heart has been deceived and hardened by the enemy. We need God's heart—a soft and responsive spiritual center that will receive the truth of God's Word.

4. Specifically, we must understand this: From God's perspective there is an indisputable connection between life and blood. In other words, if there was no blood in God's Word, there would be no testimony about life—only death! When we understand how blood literally produces life and sustains life, we can then understand *how* the application of Jesus's blood produces the life that God intends for us. We can understand *why* it is the *standard* raised against the enemy.

5. To manifest God's transformation, we die to ourselves. And we yield to the power of the Spirit, our Advocate, our Helper, our Counselor and Friend. The Spirit takes us to Jesus in the heavenly realm where He is. There, we apply His blood and receive an unlimited supply of mercy and grace, along with anything else we might need. This is how we learn to maintain a clean conscience, which keeps our receiving channels open! Our fertile hearts produce many seeds. Then—as we learn to remain in Him and freely receive the gifts of God—we transform into people who freely give! We sow into others—affirming or speaking life and blessing. We also give of our time, money, talents, and resources. Repetition, along with increase, produces a crop 30–60–100 times what we have sown! Joy spreads!

6. Jesus had mercy on the adulteress. Yes, she became clean and subsequently transformed because she received mercy in her time of

need. The encounter produced revelation concerning the magnitude of God's love and empowered her to "go and sin no more." It changed her life.

7. Jesus asked the blind man, "What can you see now?" The blind man saw people, but they looked like trees. Then Jesus laid his hands on the man again. His sight was completely restored and "he could see everything clearly."

SCRIPTURE VERSES FOR DISCUSSION QUESTIONS

Chapter 1

1. Ears to hear and eyes to see. Both are gifts from the LORD.

PROVERBS 20:12

And God saw that it was good.

GENESIS 1:10, 12

Then God blessed them. . .

GENESIS 1:22

The LORD directs the steps of the godly. He delights in every detail of their lives. Though they stumble, they will never fall, for the LORD holds them by the hand.

PSALM 37:23–24

And we know that all things work together for the good of those who love God and are called according to his purpose for them.

ROMANS 8:28

Then the LORD God said, "It is not good for the man to be alone. I will make a helper who is just right for him."

GENESIS 2:18

"For I know the plans I have for you," says the LORD. *"They are plans for good and not for disaster, to give you a future and a hope."*

JEREMIAH 29:11

Then Jesus led them to Bethany, and lifting his hands to heaven, he blessed them. While he was blessing them, he left them and was taken up to heaven.

LUKE 24:50–51

2. *The* LORD *made all sorts of trees grow up from the ground—trees that were beautiful and that produced delicious fruit. In the middle of the garden he placed the tree of life and the tree of the knowledge of good and evil.*

GENESIS 2:9

So they shall fear the name of the LORD *from the west, and his glory from the rising of the sun. When the enemy shall come in like a flood, the Spirit of the* LORD *shall lift up a standard against him.*

ISAIAH 59:19 (KJV)

Then the angel showed me a river with the water of life, clear as crystal, flowing from the throne of God and of the Lamb. It flowed down the center of the main street. On each side of the river grew a tree of life, bearing twelve crops of fruit, with a fresh crop each month. The leaves were used for medicine to heal the nations. No longer will there be a curse upon anything, for the throne of God and the Lamb will be there, and his servants will worship him. And they will see his face, and his name will be written on their foreheads. And there will be no night there—no need for lamps or sun—for the Lord God will shine on them. And they will reign forever and ever.

REVELATION 22:1–5

3. But the LORD God warned him, "You may freely eat the fruit of every tree in the garden — except the tree of the knowledge of good and evil. If you eat its fruit, you are sure to die."

GENESIS 2:16–17

4. For the Spirit of God has made me, and the breath of the Almighty gives me life.

JOB 33:4

Then God said, "Let us make human beings in our image to be like us. They will reign over the fish in the sea, the birds in the sky, the livestock, all the wild animals on the earth, and the small animals that scurry along the ground."

GENESIS 1:26

When I look at the night sky and see the work of your fingers— the moon and the stars you set in place—what are mere mortals that you should think about them, human beings that you should care for them? Yet you made them only a little lower than God and crowned them with glory and honor. You gave them charge of everything you made, putting all things under their authority.

PSALM 8:1–3

The LORD God placed the man in the Garden of Eden to tend and watch over it. But the LORD God warned him, "You may freely eat the fruit of every tree in the garden—except the tree of the knowledge of good and evil. If you eat its fruit, you are sure to die."

GENESIS 2:15–17

5. *Surely your goodness and unfailing love will pursue me all the days of my life, and I will live in the house of the LORD forever.*

PSALM 23:6

I can never escape from your Spirit! I can never get away from your presence. How precious are your thoughts about me, O God. They cannot be numbered!

PSALM 139:7, 17

But now, O Jacob, listen to the LORD who created you. O Israel, the one who formed you says, "Do not be afraid, for I have ransomed you. I have called you by name; you are mine. When you go through rivers of difficulty, you will not drown. When you walk through the fire of oppression, you will not be burned up; the flames will not consume you. For I am the LORD, your God, the Holy One of Israel, your Savior. I gave Egypt and Seba in your place. Others were given in exchange for you. I traded their lives for yours because you are precious to me. You are honored, and I love you."

ISAIAH 43:1–4

Chapter 2

1. *"The Kingdom of God is near! Repent of your sins and believe the Good news!"*

MARK 1:15

"For the mountains may move and the hills disappear, but even then my faithful love for you will remain. My covenant of blessing will never be broken," says the LORD, who has mercy on you.

ISAIAH 54:10

Dear friends, let us continue to love one another, for love comes from God. Anyone who loves is a child of God and knows God. But anyone who does not love does not know God, for God is love.

1 JOHN 4:7–8

For the LORD your God is living among you. He is a mighty savior. He will take delight in you with gladness. With his love, he will calm all your fears. He will rejoice over you with joyful songs.

ZEPHANIAH 3:17

Give thanks to the God of heaven. His faithful love endures forever.

PSALM 136:26

But you, O LORD, are a God of compassion and mercy, slow to get angry and filled with unfailing love and faithfulness.

PSALM 86:15

My child, don't reject the LORD's discipline, and don't be upset when he corrects you. For the LORD corrects those he loves, just as a father corrects a child in whom he delights.

PROVERBS 3:11–12

2. *It's your sins that have cut you off from God. Because of your sins, he has turned away and will not listen anymore.*

ISAIAH 59:2

For I was born a sinner—yes, from the moment my mother conceived me.

PSALM 51:5

All of us like, like sheep, have gone astray. We have left God's paths to follow our own. Yet the LORD laid on him the sins of us all.

ISAIAH 53:6

3. *The Lord isn't really being slow about his promise, as some people think. No, his is being patient for your sake. He does not want anyone to be destroyed, but wants everyone to repent.*

2 PETER 3:9

"In a burst of anger, I turned my face away for a little while. But with everlasting love I will have compassion on you," says the LORD, your Redeemer.

ISAIAH 54:8

The sacrifice you desire is a broken spirit. You will not reject a broken and repentant heart, O God.

PSALM 51:17

This is the message we have heard from Jesus and now declare to you: God is light, and there is no darkness in him at all. So we are lying if we say we have fellowship with God but go on living in spiritual darkness; we are not practicing the truth. But if we are living in the light, as God is in the light, then we have fellowship with each other, and the blood of Jesus, his Son, cleanses us from all sin.

1 JOHN 1:5–7

"If you look for me wholeheartedly, you will find me. I will be found by you," says the LORD. "I will end your captivity and restore your fortunes. I will gather you out of the nations where I sent you and will bring you home again to your own land."

JEREMIAH 29:13–14

For the kind of sorrow God wants us to experience leads us away from sin and results in salvation. There's no regret for that kind of sorrow. But worldly sorrow, which lacks repentance, results in spiritual death.

2 Corinthians 7:10

Don't you see how wonderfully kind, tolerant, and patient God is with you? Does this mean nothing to you? Can't you see that his kindness is intended to turn you from your sin? But because you are stubborn and refuse to turn from your sin, you are storing up terrible punishment for yourself. For a day of anger is coming, when God's righteous judgment will be revealed.

Romans 2:4–5

4. *Notice how God is both kind and severe. His is severe toward those who disobeyed, but kind to you if you continue to trust in his kindness. But if you stop trusting, you also will be cut off.*

Romans 11:22

For the wages of sin is death, but the free gift of God is eternal life through Christ Jesus our Lord.

Romans 6:23

Chapter 3

1. *To all who believed Him and accepted Him, He gave the right to become children of God.*

John 1:12

All right then, the Lord himself will give you the sign. Look! The virgin will conceive a child! She will give birth to a son and will call him Immanuel (which means 'God is with us').

Isaiah 7:14, Matthew 1:23

For the life of the body is in its blood. I have given you the blood on the altar to purify you, making you right with the Lord. It is the blood, given in exchange for a life that makes purification possible.

LEVITICUS 17:11

2. *If any of your fellow Israelites fall into poverty and are forced to sell themselves to such a foreigner or to a member of his family, they still retain the right to be bought back, even after they have been purchased. They will negotiate the price of their freedom with the person who bought them.*

LEVITICUS 25:47–54

His is so rich in kindness and grace that he purchased our freedom with the blood of his Son and forgave our sins.

EPHESIANS 1:7

With his own blood – not the blood of goats and calves—he entered the Most Holy Place once for all time and secured our redemption forever.

HEBREWS 9:12

We also know that the Son did not come to help angels; he came to help the descendants of Abraham. Therefore, it was necessary for him to be made in every respect like us, his brothers and sisters, so that he could be our merciful and faithful High Priest before God. Then he could offer a sacrifice that would take away the sins of the people.

HEBREWS 2:16–17

If that had been necessary, Christ would have had to die again and again, ever since the world began. But now, once for all time, he has appeared at the end of the age to remove sin by his own death as a sacrifice.

HEBREWS 9:26

"I—yes, I alone—will blot out your sins for my own sake and will never think of them again."

ISAIAH 43:25

3. *If you confess with your mouth that Jesus is Lord and believe in your heart that God raised him from the dead, you will be saved. For it is by believing in your heart that you are made right with God, and it is by confessing with your mouth that you are saved.*

ROMANS 10:9–10

4. *Faith is the confidence that what we hope for will actually happen; it gives us assurance about things we cannot see.*

HEBREWS 11:1

So faith comes from hearing that is, hearing the Good News about Christ.

ROMANS 10:17

5. *But to all who believed him and accepted him, he gave the right to become children of God. They are reborn — not with a physical birth resulting from human passion or plan, but a birth that comes from God.*

JOHN 1:12–13

There was a man named Nicodemus, a Jewish religious leader who was a Pharisee. After dark one evening, he came to speak with Jesus. "Rabbi," he said, "we all know that God has sent you to

*teach us. Your miraculous signs are evidence that God is with you."
Jesus replied, "I tell you the truth, unless you are born again, you
cannot see the Kingdom of God." "What do you mean?" exclaimed
Nicodemus. "How can an old man go back into his mother's womb
and be born again?" Jesus replied, "I assure you, no one can enter
the Kingdom of God without being born of water and the Spirit.
Humans can reproduce only human life, but the Holy Spirit gives
birth to spiritual life. So don't be surprised when I say, 'You must
be born again.' The wind blows where it wants. Just as you can hear
the wind but can't tell where it comes from or where it is going, so
you can't explain how people are born of the Spirit."*

JOHN 3:1–8

*And I will give you a new heart, and I will put a new spirit in you.
I will take out your stony, stubborn heart and give you a tender,
responsive heart. And I will put my Spirit in you so that you will
follow my decrees and be careful to obey my regulations.*

EZEKIEL 36:26–27

*Jesus told him, "I am the way, the truth, and the life. No one can
come to the Father except through me. If you had really known me,
you would know who my Father is. From now on, you do know him
and have seen him!"*

JOHN 14:6–7

*Yes, Adam's one sin brings condemnation for everyone, but Christ's
one act of righteousness brings a right relationship with God and
new life for everyone.*

ROMANS 5:18

*The apostles said to the Lord, "Show us how to increase our faith."
The Lord answered, "If you had faith even as small as a mustard
seed, you could say to this mulberry tree, 'May you be uprooted and
thrown into the sea,' and it would obey you!"*

LUKE 17:5–6

*"What do you mean, 'If I can'?" Jesus asked. "Anything is possible if
a person believes." The father instantly cried out, "I do believe, but
help me overcome my unbelief!" When Jesus saw that the crowd of
onlookers was growing, he rebuked the evil spirit. "Listen, you spirit
that makes this boy unable to hear and speak," he said. "I command
you to come out of this child and never enter him again!"*

MARK 9:23–25

Chapter 4

1. *Then Jesus uttered another loud cry and breathed his last. And the
curtain in the sanctuary of the Temple was torn in two, from top to
bottom.*

MARK 15:37–38

*At noon, darkness fell across the whole land until three o'clock. At
about three o'clock, Jesus called out with a loud voice, "Eli, Eli,
lema sabachthani?" which means "my God, my God, why have
you abandoned me?". . .Then Jesus shouted out again, and he
released his spirit. At that moment the curtain in the sanctuary of
the Temple was torn in two, from top to bottom. The earth shook,
rocks split apart, and tombs opened. The bodies of many godly
men and women who had died were raised from the dead. They left
the cemetery after Jesus' resurrection, went into the holy city of
Jerusalem, and appeared to many people.*

MATTHEW 27:45–46, 50–53

2. *The old system under the law of Moses was only a shadow, a dim*
   preview of the good thing to come, not the good things themselves.
   The sacrifices under that system were repeated again and again,
   year after year, but they were never able to provide perfect cleansing
   for those who came to worship. If they could have provided perfect
   cleansing, the sacrifices would have stopped, for the worshipers
   would have been purified once for all time, and their feelings of
   guilt would have disappeared. But instead, those sacrifices actually
   reminded them of their sins year after year. For it is not possible for
   the blood of bulls and goats to take away sins.

   HEBREWS 10:1–5

Mary was standing outside the tomb crying, and as she wept, she
stooped and looked in. She saw two white–robed angels, one sitting
at the head and the other at the foot of the place where the body
of Jesus had been lying. "Dear woman, why are you crying?" the
angels asked her. "Because they have taken away my Lord," she
replied. "And I don't know where they have put him." She turned to
leave and saw someone standing there. It was Jesus, but she didn't
recognize him. "Dear woman, why are you crying?" Jesus asked her.
"Who are you looking for?" She thought he was the gardener. "Sir,"
she said, "if you have taken him away, tell me where you have put
him, and I will go and get him." "Mary!" Jesus said. She turned
to him and cried out, "Rabboni!" (which is Hebrew for "Teacher").
"Don't cling to me," Jesus said, "for I have yet to ascend to the
Father. But go find my brothers and tell them, 'I am ascending
to my Father and your Father, to my God and your God.'" Mary
Magdalene found the disciples and told them, "I have seen the
Lord!" Then she gave them his message.

JOHN 20:11–18

So Christ has now become the High Priest over all the good things that have come. He has entered that greater, more perfect Tabernacle in heaven, which was not made by human hands and is not part of this created world. With his own blood — not the blood of goats and calves — he entered the Most Holy Place once for all time and secured our redemption forever.

HEBREWS 9:11–12

3. *Then he breathed on them and said, "Receive the Holy Spirit."*

JOHN 20:22

"And now I will send the Holy Spirit, just as my Father promised. But stay here in the city until the Holy Spirit comes and fills you with power from heaven."

LUKE 24:49

4. *Here is the main point: We have a High Priest who sat down in the place of honor beside the throne of the majestic God in heaven. There he ministers in the heavenly Tabernacle, the true place of worship that was built by the Lord and not by human hands.*

HEBREWS 8:1–2

Therefore he is able, once and forever, to save those who come to God through him. He lives forever to intercede with God on their behalf.

HEBREWS 7:25

Now he is exalted to the place of highest honor in heaven, at God's right hand. And the Father, as he had promised, gave him the Holy Spirit to pour out upon us, just as you see and hear today.

ACTS 2:33

5. *We now have this light shining in our hearts, but we ourselves are
   like fragile clay jars containing this great treasure. This makes it
   clear that our great power is from God, not from ourselves.*

   2 CORINTHIANS 4:7

*Each time he said, "My grace is all you need. My power works best
in weakness. So now I am glad to boast about my weaknesses, so
that the power of Christ can work through me.*

2 CORINTHIANS 12:9

*Now all glory to God, who is able, through his mighty power at
work within us, to accomplish infinitely more than we might ask or
think. Glory to him in the church and in Christ Jesus through all
generations forever and ever! Amen.*

EPHESIANS 3:20–21

*For God has not given us a spirit of fear and timidity, but of power,
love, and self–discipline.*

2 TIMOTHY 1:7

*"Teacher, what is the most important commandment in the law of
Moses?" Jesus replied, "'You must love the Lord your God with all
your heart, all your soul, and all your mind.' This is the first and
greatest commandment. A second is equally important: 'Love your
neighbor as yourself.' The entire law and all the demands of the
prophets are based on these two commandments."*

MATTHEW 22:36–40

*"So now I give you a new commandment: Love each other. Just
as I have loved you, you should love each other. Your love for one*

another will prove to the world that you are my disciples."

JOHN 13:34–35

"Those who accept my commandments and obey them are the ones who love me. And because they love me, my Father will love them. And I will love them and reveal myself to each of them."

JOHN 14:21

The purpose of my instruction is that all believers would be filled with love that comes from a pure heart, a clear conscience, and genuine faith.

1 TIMOTHY 1:5

And this hope will not lead to disappointment. For we know how dearly God loves us, because he has given us the Holy Spirit to fill our hearts with his love.

ROMANS 5:5

Then Christ will make his home in your hearts as you trust him. Your roots will grow down into God's love and keep you strong.

EPHESIANS 3:17

6. *When he appeared in human form, he humbled himself in obedience to God and died a criminal's death on a cross.*

PHILIPPIANS 2:8

For God is working in you, giving you the desire and the power to do what pleases him.

PHILIPPIANS 2:13

7. *But the person who is joined to the Lord is one spirit with him.*

1 CORINTHIANS 6:17

Chapter 5

1. *For God's will was for us to be made holy by the sacrifice of the body of Jesus Christ, once for all time.*

HEBREWS 10:10

Make them holy by your truth; teach them your word, which is truth. Just as you sent me into the world, I am sending them into the world. And I give myself as a holy sacrifice for them so they can be made holy by your truth.

JOHN 17:17–19

By his divine power, God has given us everything we need for living a godly life. We have received all of this by coming to know him, the one who called us to himself by means of his marvelous glory and excellence. And because of his glory and excellence, he has given us great and precious promises. These are the promises that enable you to share his divine nature and escape the world's corruption caused by human desires.

2 PETER 1:3–4

2. *I pray for you constantly, asking God, the glorious Father of our Lord Jesus Christ, to give you spiritual wisdom and insight so that you might grow in your knowledge of God. I pray that your hearts will be flooded with light so that you can understand the confident hope he has given to those he called — his holy people who are his rich and glorious inheritance. I also pray that you will understand the incredible greatness of God's power for us who believe him. This is the same mighty power that raised Christ from the dead and seated him in the place of honor at God's right hand in the heavenly realms. Now he is far above any ruler or authority or power or*

leader or anything else — not in this world but also in the world to come. God has put all things under the authority of Christ and has made him head over all things for the benefit of the church. And the church is his body; it is made full and complete by Christ, who fills all things everywhere with himself.

EPHESIANS 1:17–23

Since you have heard about Jesus and have learned the truth that comes from him, throw off your old sinful nature and your former way of life, which is corrupted by lust and deception. Instead, let the Spirit renew your thoughts and attitudes. Put on your new nature, created to be like God—truly righteous and holy.

EPHESIANS 4:21–24

"Make them holy by your truth; teach them your word, which is truth."

JOHN 17:17

3. *Let us go into the presence of God with sincere hearts fully trusting him. For our guilty consciences have been sprinkled with Christ's blood to make us clean, and our bodies have been washed with pure water.*

HEBREWS 10:22

For the word of God is alive and powerful. It is sharper than the sharpest two-edged sword, cutting between soul and spirit, between joint and marrow. It exposes our innermost thoughts and desires.

HEBREWS 4:12

4. *"Yes, I am the gate. Those who come in through me will be saved. They will come and go freely and find good pastures."*

JOHN 10:9

5. But to all who received him and accepted him, he gave the right to
become children of God.

JOHN 1:12

Adam was the son of God.

LUKE 3:38

Let all that I am praise the LORD; with my whole heart, I will praise
his holy name. Let all that I am praise the LORD; may I never forget
the good things he does for me. He forgives all my sins and heals
all my diseases. He redeems me from death and crowns me with love
and tender mercies. He fills my life with good things. My youth is
renewed like the eagle's!

PSALM 103:1–5

6. "For I know the plans I have for you, says the LORD. "They are plans
for good and not for disaster, to give you a future and a hope. For
in those days when you pray, I will listen. If you look for me wholeheartedly, you will find me. I will be found by you," says the LORD.

JEREMIAH 29:11–13

"So if the Son sets you free, you are truly free."

JOHN 8:36

May the LORD bless you and protect you. May the LORD smile on you
and be gracious to you. May the LORD show you his favor and give
you his peace.

NUMBERS 6:24–26

For since the world began, no ear has heard and no eye has seen a God like you, who works for those who wait for him!

ISAIAH 64:4

But you, oh LORD, are a shield around me; you are my glory, the one who holds my head high.

PSALM 3:3

You will keep in perfect peace all who trust in you, all whose thoughts are fixed on you!

ISAIAH 26:3

You go before me and follow me. You place your hand of blessing on my head.

PSALM 139:5

For he has rescued us from the kingdom of darkness and transferred us into the Kingdom of his dear Son, who purchased our freedom and forgave our sins.

COLOSSIANS 1:13–14

So humble yourselves under the mighty power of God, and at the right time he will lift you up in honor. Give all your worries and cares to God, for he cares about you.

1 PETER 5:6–7

7. *"For you are the children of your father the devil, and you love to do the evil things he does. He was a murderer from the beginning. He has always hated the truth, because there is no truth in him. When he lies, it is consistent with his character; for he is a liar and the father of lies."*

JOHN 8:44

Once you were dead, because of your disobedience and your many sins. You used to live in sin, just like the rest of the world, obeying the devil — the commander of the powers in the unseen world. He is the spirit at work in the hearts of those who refuse to obey God.

EPHESIANS 2:1–2

If the Good News we preach is hidden behind a veil, it is hidden only from people who are perishing. Satan, who is the god of this world, has blinded the minds of those who don't believe. They are unable to see the glorious light of the Good News. They don't understand this message about the glory of Christ, who is the exact likeness of God.

2 CORINTHIANS 4:3–4

This great dragon — the ancient serpent called the devil, or Satan, the deceiving the whole world — was thrown down to the earth with all his angels. Then I heard a loud voice shouting across the heavens, "It has come at last — salvation and power and the Kingdom of our God, and the authority of his Christ. For the accuser of our brothers and sisters has been thrown down to earth — the one who accuses them before our God day and night. . . . Therefore, rejoice, O heavens! And you who live in the heavens, rejoice! But terror will come on the earth and the sea, for the devil has come down to you in great anger, knowing that he has little time."

REVELATION 12:9–10, 12

Stay alert! Watch out for your great enemy, the devil. He prowls around like a roaring lion, looking for someone to devour.

1 PETER 5:8

Yet when I am among mature believers, I do speak with words of wisdom, but not the kind of wisdom that belongs to this world or to the rulers of this world, who are soon forgotten. No, the wisdom we speak of is the mystery of God — his plan that was previously hidden, even though he made it for our ultimate glory before the world began. But the rulers of this world have not understood it; if they had, they would not have crucified our glorious Lord. That is what the Scriptures mean when they say, "No eye has seen, no ear has heard, and no mind has imagined what God has prepared for those who love him." But it was to us that God revealed these things by his Spirit, for his Spirit searches out everything and shows us God's deep secrets. No one can know a person's thoughts except that person's own spirit, and no one can know God's thoughts except God's own Spirit. And we have received God's Spirit (not the world's spirit), so we can know the wonderful things God has freely given us. When we tell you these things, we do not use words that come from human wisdom. Instead, we speak words given to us by the Spirit, using the Spirit's words to explain spiritual truths. But people who aren't spiritual can't receive these truths from God's Spirit. It all sounds foolish to them and they can't understand it, for only those who are spiritual can understand what the Spirit means. Those who are spiritual can evaluate all things, but they themselves cannot be evaluated by others. For "Who can know the Lord's thoughts? Who knows enough to teach him?" But we understand these things, for we have the mind of Christ.

1 CORINTHIANS 2:6–16

Chapter 6

1. *But the Son of God came to destroy the works of the Devil.*

1 JOHN 3:8

*So now there is no condemnation for those who belong to Christ
Jesus. And because you belong to him, the power of the life—giving
Spirit has freed you from the power of sin that leads to death. The
law of Moses was unable to save us because of the weakness of our
sinful nature. So God did what the law could not do. He sent his
own Son in a body like the bodies we sinners have. And in that body
God declared an end to sin's control over us by giving his Son as a
sacrifice for our sins. He did this so that the just requirement of the
law would be fully satisfied for us, who no longer follow our sinful
nature but instead follow the Spirit.*

ROMANS 8:1—4

2. *So you have not received a spirit that makes you fearful slaves.
Instead, you received God's Spirit when he adopted you as his own
children. Now we call him, "Abba, Father."*

ROMANS 8:15

*Jesus traveled through all the towns and villages of that area,
teaching in the synagogues and announcing the Good News about
the Kingdom. And he healed every kind of disease and illness.
When he saw the crowds, he had compassion on them because they
were confused and helpless, like sheep without a shepherd. He said
to his disciples, "The harvest is great, but the workers are few. So
pray to the Lord who is in charge of the harvest; ask him to send
more workers into his fields."*

MATTHEW 9:35—38

*Jesus entered Jericho and made his way through the town. There
was a man there named Zacchaeus. He was the chief tax collector
in the region, and he had become very rich. He tried to get a look*

at Jesus, but he was too short to see over the crowd. So he ran ahead and climbed a sycamore–fig tree beside the road, for Jesus was going to pass that way. When Jesus came by, he looked up at Zacchaeus and called him by name. "Zacchaeus!" he said. "Quick, come down! I must be a guest in your home today." Zacchaeus quickly climbed down and took Jesus to his house in great excitement and joy. But the people were displeased. "He has gone to be the guest of a notorious sinner," they grumbled. Meanwhile Zacchaeus stood before the Lord and said, I will give half my wealth to the poor, Lord, and if I have cheated people on their taxes, I will give them back four times as much!" Jesus responded, "Salvation has come to this home today, for this man has shown himself to be a true son of Abraham. For the Son of Man came to seek and save those who are lost."

LUKE 19:1–10

Jesus climbed into a boat and went back across the lake to his own town. Some people brought to him a paralyzed man on a mat. Seeing their faith, Jesus said to the paralyzed man, "Be encouraged, my child! Your sins are forgiven." But some of the teachers of religious law said to themselves, "That's blasphemy! Does he think he's God?" Jesus knew what they were thinking, so he asked them, "Why do you have such evil thought in your hearts? Is it easier to say 'Your sins are forgiven,' or 'Stand up and walk'? So I will prove to you that the Son of Man has authority on earth to forgive sins." Then Jesus turned to the paralyzed man and said, "Stand up, pick up your mat, and go home!" And the man jumped up and went home! Fear swept through the crowd as they saw this happen. And they praised God for sending a man with such great authority.

MATTHEW 9:1–8

*As Jesus approached Jericho, a blind beggar was sitting beside the
road. When he heard the noise of a crowd going past, he asked what
was happening. They told him that Jesus the Nazarene was going
by. So he began shouting, "Jesus, Son of David, have mercy on me!"
When Jesus heard him, he stopped and ordered that the man be
brought to him. As the man came near, Jesus asked him, "What do
you want me to do for you?" "Lord," he said, "I want to see!" And
Jesus said, "All right, receive your sight! Your faith has healed you."
Instantly the man could see, and he followed Jesus, praising God.
And all who saw it praised God, too.*

LUKE 18:35–42

*Just then a woman who had suffered for twelve years with constant
bleeding came up behind him. She touched the fringe of his robe,
for she thought, "If I can just touch his robe, I will be healed."
Jesus turned around, and when he saw her he said, "Daughter, be
encouraged! Your faith has made you well." And the woman was
healed at that moment.*

MATTHEW 9:20–22

*Then those who had seen what happened told the others how the
demon–possessed man had been healed.*

LUKE 8:36

3. *Jesus called his twelve disciples together and gave them authority to
cast out evil spirits and to heal every kind of disease and illness.*

MATTHEW 10:1

*The Lord now chose seventy–two other disciples and sent them ahead
in pairs to all the towns and places he planned to visit. These were
his instructions to them: "The harvest is great, but the workers are*

few. So pray to the Lord who is in charge of the harvest; ask him to send more workers into his fields. Now go, and remember that I am sending you out as lambs among wolves. Don't take any money with you, nor a traveler's bag, nor an extra pair of sandals. And don't stop to greet anyone on the road. Whenever you enter someone's home, first say, 'May God's peace be on this house.' If those who live there are peaceful, the blessing will stand; if they are not, the blessing will return to you. Don't move around from home to home. Stay in one place, eating and drinking what they provide. Don't hesitate to accept hospitality, because those who work deserve their pay. If you enter a town and it welcomes you, eat whatever is set before you. Heal the sick and tell them, 'The Kingdom of God is near you now.'

LUKE 10:1–10

As it happened, Publius's father was ill with fever and dysentery. Paul went in and prayed for him, and laying his hands on him, he healed him. Then all the other sick people on the island came and were healed.

ACTS 28:8–9

"I tell you the truth, anyone who believes in me will do the same works I have done, and even greater works, because I am going to be with the Father. You can ask for anything in my name, and I will do it, so that the Son can bring glory to the Father. Yes, ask me for anything in my name, and I will do it!"

JOHN 14:12

I also pray that you will understand the incredible greatness of God's power for us who believe him. This is the same mighty power that raised Christ from the dead and seated him in the place of honor at God's right hand in the heavenly realms. Now he is far

*above any ruler or authority or power or leader or anything else —
not only in this world but also in the world to come. God has put
all things under the authority of Christ and has made him head
over all things for the benefit of the church. And the church is his
body; it is made full and complete by Christ, who fills all things
everywhere with himself.*

EPHESIANS 1:19–22

*Are any of you suffering hardships? You should pray. Are any of you
happy? You should sing praises. Are any of you sick? You should call for
the elders of the church to come and pray over you, anointing you with
oil in the name of the Lord. Such a prayer offered in faith will heal the
sick, and the Lord will make you well. And if you have committed any
sins, you will be forgiven. Confess your sins to each other and pray for
each other so that you may be healed. The earnest prayer of a righteous
person has great power and produces wonderful results.*

JAMES 5:13–16

4. *I tell you the truth, whatever you forbid (bind or lock) on earth will
   be forbidden in heaven, and whatever you permit (loose or open) on
   earth will be permitted in heaven.*

MATTHEW 18:18

*For we are not fighting against flesh—and—blood enemies, but against
evil rulers and authorities of the unseen world, against mighty powers
in this dark world, and against evil spirits in the heavenly places.*

EPHESIANS 6:12

5. *The thief's purpose is to steal and kill and destroy. My purpose is to
   give them a rich and satisfying life.*

JOHN 10:10

And this is what God has testified: He has given us eternal life, and this life is in his Son. Whoever has the Son has life; whoever does not have God's Son does not have life.

1 JOHN 5:11–12

Dear friends, since God loved us that much, we surely ought to love each other. No one has ever seen God. But if we love each other, God lives in us, and his love is brought to full expression in us. And God has given us his Spirit as proof that we live in him and he in us.

1 JOHN 4:11–13

He redeems me from death and crowns me with love and tender mercies.

PSALM 103:4

Now Christ has gone to heaven. He is seated in the place of honor next to God, and all the angels and authorities and powers accept his authority.

1 PETER 3:22

6. *And they sang a new song with these words: "You are worthy to take the scroll and break its seals and open it. For you were slaughtered, and your blood has ransomed people for God from every tribe and language and people and nation. And you have caused them to become a Kingdom of priests for our God. And they will reign on the earth."*

REVELATION 5:9–10

But you are not like that, for you are a chosen people. You are royal priests, a holy nation, God's very own possession. As a result, you can show others the goodness of God, for he called you out of the darkness into his wonderful light.

1 PETER 2:9

For the sin of this one man, Adam, caused death to rule over many. But even greater is God's wonderful grace and his gift of righteousness, for all who receive it will live in triumph over sin and death through this one man, Jesus Christ.

ROMANS 5:17

John replied, "No one can receive anything unless God gives it from heaven. You yourselves know how plainly I told you,' I am not the Messiah. I am only here to prepare the way for him.' It is the bridegroom who marries the bride, and the best man is simply glad to stand with him and hear his vows. Therefore, I am filled with joy at his success. He must become greater and greater, and I must become less and less.

JOHN 3:27–30

But you belong to God, my dear children. You have already won a victory over those people, because the Spirit who lives in you is greater than the spirit who lives in the world.

1 JOHN 4:4

Chapter 7

1. *"The Kingdom of Heaven is like a treasure that a man discovered hidden in a field. In his excitement, he hid it again and sold everything he owned to get enough money to buy the field."*

MATTHEW 13:44

2. *For the Kingdom of God is not a matter of what we eat or drink but of living a life of goodness and peace and joy in the Holy Spirit.*

ROMANS 14:17

Later on, after John was arrested, Jesus went into Galilee, where he preached God's Good News. "The time promised by God has come at last!" he announced. "The Kingdom of God is near! Repent of your sins and believe the Good News!"

MARK 1:14–15

"When will the Kingdom of God come?" Jesus replied, "The Kingdom of God can't be detected by visible signs. You won't be able to say, 'Here it is!' or 'It's over there!' For the Kingdom of God is already among you." (i.e. the Kingdom is within you, or is in your grasp.)

LUKE 17:20–21 (AMPLIFIED BIBLE AMP)

3. *"For everything that is hidden will eventually be brought into the open, and every secret will be brought to light. Anyone with ears to hear should listen and understand." Then he added, "Pay close attention to what you hear. The closer you listen the more under-standing you will be given — and you will receive even more."*

MARK 4:22–24

But it was to us that God revealed these things by his Spirit. For his Spirit searches out everything and shows us God's deep secrets. No one can know a person's thoughts except that person's own spirit, and no one can know God's thoughts except God's own Spirit. And we have received God's Spirit (not the world's spirit), so we can know the wonderful things God has freely given us.

1 CORINTHIANS 2:10–12

4. *"I have told you these things so you will be filled with my joy. Yes, your joy will overflow!"*

JOHN 15:11

For the Lord grants wisdom! From his mouth come knowledge and understanding. He grants a treasure of common sense to the honest. He is a shield to those who walk with integrity. He guards the paths of the just and protects those who are faithful to him. Then you will understand what is right, just, and fair, and you will find the right way to go. For wisdom will enter your heart, and knowledge will fill you with joy. Wise choices will watch over you. Understanding will keep you safe. Wisdom will save you from evil people, from those whose words are twisted.

PROVERBS 2:6–12

5. *Study this Book of Instruction continually. Meditate on it day and night so you will be sure to obey everything written in it. Only then will you prosper and succeed in all you do.*

JOSHUA 1:8

For the word of God is alive and powerful. It is sharper than the sharpest two–edged sword, cutting between soul and spirit, between joint and marrow. It exposes our innermost thoughts and desires.

HEBREWS 4:12

The tongue can bring death or life: those who love to talk will reap the consequences.

PROVERBS 18:21

"The words you say will either acquit you or condemn you."

MATTHEW 12:37

"A good person produces good things from the treasury of a good heart, and an evil person produces evil things from the treasury of an evil heart. What you say flows from what is in your heart."

LUKE 6:45

No, the message is very close at hand; it is on your lips and in your heart so that you can obey it.

DEUTERONOMY 30:14

6. *When the seventy—two disciples returned, they joyfully reported to him, "Lord, even the demons obey us when we use your name!" "Yes, he told them, "I saw Satan fall from heaven like lightning! Look, I have given you authority over all the power of the enemy, and you can walk among snakes and scorpions and crush them. Nothing will injure you. But don't rejoice because evil spirits obey you; rejoice because your names are registered in heaven." At that same time Jesus was filled with the joy of the Holy Spirit, and he said, "O Father, Lord of heaven and earth, thank you for hiding these things from those who think themselves wise and clever, and revealing them to the childlike. Yes, Father, it pleased you to do it this way. My Father has entrusted everything to me. No one truly knows the Son except the Father, and no one truly knows the Father except the Son and those to whom the Son chooses to reveal him." Then when they were alone, he turned to the disciples and said, "Blessed are the eyes that see what you have seen. I tell you, many prophets and kings longed to see what you see, but they didn't see it. And they longed to hear what you hear, but they didn't hear it."*

LUKE 10:17–23

7. *"You haven't done this before. Ask, using my name, and you will receive, and you will have abundant joy."*

JOHN 16:24

"Yes, I am the vine; you are the branches. Those who remain in me, and I in them, will produce much fruit. For apart from me you can do nothing. Anyone who does not remain in me is thrown away like a useless branch and withers. Such branches are gathered into pile

to be burned. But if you remain in me and my words remain in you, you may ask for anything you want, and it will be granted! When you produce much fruit, you are my true disciples. This brings great glory to my Father."

JOHN 15:5–8

Let all that I am praise the LORD; may I never forget the good things he does for me. He forgives all my sins and heals all my diseases. He redeems me from death and crowns me with love and tender mercies. He fills my life with good things. My youth is renewed like the eagle's!

PSALM 103:2–5

And this same God who takes care of me will supply all your needs from his glorious riches, which have been given to us in Christ Jesus.

PHILIPPIANS 4:19

Chapter 8

1. *There is a path before each person that seems right, but it ends in death.*

PROVERBS 14:12

"The thief's purpose is to steal and kill and destroy. My purpose is to give them a rich and satisfying life."

JOHN 10:10

"But I will send you the Advocate—the Spirit of truth. He will come to you from the Father and will testify all about me."

JOHN 16:24

Jesus returned to the Mount of Olives, but early the next morning he was back again at the Temple. A crowd soon gathered, and he sat down and taught them. As he was speaking, the teachers of religious law and the Pharisees brought a woman who had been caught in the act of adultery. They put her in front of the crowd. "Teacher," they said to Jesus, "this woman was caught in the act of adultery. The law of Moses says to stone her. What do you say?" They were trying to trap him into saying something they could use against him, but Jesus stooped down and wrote in the dust with his finger. They kept demanding an answer, so he stood up again and said, "All right, but let the one who has never sinned throw the first stone!" Then he stooped down again and wrote in the dust. When the accusers heard this, they slipped away one by one, beginning with the oldest, until only Jesus was left in the middle of the crowd with the woman. Then Jesus stood up again and said to the woman, "Where are your accusers? Didn't even one of them condemn you?" "No, Lord," she said. And Jesus said, "Neither do I. Go and sin no more."

JOHN 8:1–11

For God has not given us a spirit of fear and timidity, but of power, love, and self–discipline.

2 TIMOTHY 1:7

For God is not a God of disorder but of peace, as in all the meetings of God's holy people.

1 CORINTHIANS 14:33

We are human, but we don't wage war as humans do. We use God's mighty weapons, not worldly weapons, to knock down the strongholds of human reasoning and to destroy false arguments. We destroy every proud obstacle that keeps people from knowing God. We capture their rebellious thoughts and teach them to obey Christ.

2 Corinthians 10:3–5

"My sheep listen to my voice; I know them, and they follow me. I give them eternal life, and they will never perish. No one can snatch them away from me, for my Father has given them to me, and he is more powerful than anyone else. No one can snatch them from the Father's hand. The Father and I are one."

John 10:27–30

2. *And they have defeated him by the blood of the Lamb and by their testimony. And they did not love their lives so much that they were afraid to die.*

Revelation 12:11

3. *And I will give you a new heart, and I will put a new spirit in you. I will take out your stony, stubborn heart and give you a tender, responsive heart.*

Ezekiel 36:26

The human heart is the most deceitful of all things, and desperately wicked. Who really knows how bad it is?

Jeremiah 17:9

4. *For the life of the body is in its blood. I have given you the blood on the altar to purify you, making you right with the Lord. It is the*

blood, given in exchange for a life, that makes purification possible.

LEVITICUS 17:11

5. *"I tell you the truth, unless a kernel of wheat is planted in the soil and dies, it remains alone. But its death will produce many new kernels—a plentiful harvest of new lives. Those who love their life in this world will lose it. Those who care nothing for their life in this world will keep it for eternity. Anyone who wants to be my disciple must follow me, because my servants must be where I am. And the Father will honor anyone who serves me."*

JOHN 12:24–26

"And I will ask the Father, and he will give you another Advocate, who will never leave you."

JOHN 14:16

"But when the Father sends the Advocate as my representative— that is, the Holy Spirit—he will teach you everything and will remind you of everything I have told you."

JOHN 14:26

And so, dear brothers and sisters, we can boldly enter heaven's Most Holy Place because of the blood of Jesus. By his death, Jesus opened a new and life–giving way through the curtain into the Most Holy Place. And since we have a great High Priest who rules over God's house, let us go right into the presence of God with sincere hearts fully trusting him. For our guilty consciences have been sprinkled with Christ's blood to make us clean and our bodies have been washed with pure water.

HEBREWS 10:19–22

For he raised us from the dead along with Christ and seated us with him in the heavenly realms because we are united with Christ Jesus. So God can point to us in all future ages as examples of the incredible wealth of his grace and kindness toward us, as shown in all he has done for us who are united with Christ Jesus.

EPHESIANS 2:6–7

So let us come boldly to the throne of our gracious God. There we will receive his mercy, and we will find grace to help us when we need it most.

HEBREWS 4:16

"Heal the sick, raise the dead, cure those with leprosy, and cast out demons. Give as freely as you have received!"

MATTHEW 10:8

"Still other seeds fell on fertile soil, and they produced a crop that was thirty, sixty, and even a hundred times as much as had been planted!"

MATTHEW 13:8

"The seed that fell on fertile soil represents those who truly hear and understand God's word and produce a harvest of thirty, sixty, or even a hundred times as much as had been planted!"

MATTHEW 13:23

"Give, and you will receive. Your gift will return to you in full— pressed down, shaken together to make room for more, running over, and poured into your lap. The amount you give will determine the amount you get back."

LUKE 6:38

6. *Jesus returned to the Mount of Olives, but early the next morning he was back again the Temple. A crowd soon gathered, and he sat down and taught them. As he was speaking, the teachers of religious law and the Pharisees brought a woman who had been caught in the act of adultery. They put her in front of the crowd. "Teacher," they said to Jesus, "this woman was caught in the act of adultery. The law of Moses says to stone her. What do you say?" They were trying to trap him into saying something they could use against him, but Jesus stooped down and wrote in the dust with his finger. They kept demanding an answer, so he stood up again and said, "All right, but let the one who has never sinned throw the first stone!" Then he stooped down again and wrote in the dust. When the accusers heard this, they slipped away one by one, beginning with the oldest, until only Jesus was left in the middle of the crowd with the woman. Then Jesus stood up again and said to the woman, "Where are your accusers? Didn't even one of them condemn you?" "No, Lord," she said. And Jesus said, "Neither do I. Go and sin no more."*

JOHN 8:1–11

7. *When they arrived at Bethsaida, some people brought a blind man to Jesus, and they begged him to touch the man and heal him. Jesus took the blind man by the hand and led him out of the village. Then, spitting on the man's eyes, he laid his hands on him and asked, "Can you see anything now?" the man looked around. "Yes," he said. "I see people, but I can't see them very clearly. They look like trees walking around." The Jesus placed his hands on the man's eyes again, and his eyes were opened. His sight was completely restored, and he could see everything clearly. Jesus sent him away, saying, "Don't go back into the village on your way home." Jesus and his disciples left Galilee and went up to the villages near Caesarea Philippi. As they were walking along, he asked them, "Who do people say I am?" "Well," they replied, "some say John the Baptist, some say*

Elijah, and others say you are one of the other prophets." Then he asked them, "But who do you say I am?" Peter replied, "You are the Messiah." But Jesus warned them not to tell anyone about him.

MARK 8:22–3